MW01241007

My Walk Past Hell
Vol. 2-The Men

COMPILED BY
Dr. Yolanda Jerry

© 2022 Dr. Yolanda Jerry

ISBN: 9798796408124

Book Cover Design: T.M. CREATIVE- Tanya M. Lewis

Interior Book Design & Formatting: TamikaINK.com

Editor: Tamikalnk.com

ALL RIGHTS RESERVED. No part of this book may be reproduced in any written, electronic, recording, or photocopying without written permission of the publisher or author. The exception would be in the case of brief quotations embodied in the critical articles or reviews and pages where permission is specifically granted by the publisher or author.

LEGAL DISCLAIMER. Although the author has made every effort to ensure that the information in this book was correct at press time, the author do not assume and hereby disclaim any liability to any party for any loss, damage, or disruption caused by errors or omissions, whether such errors or omissions result from negligence, accident, or any other cause.

Library of Congress Cataloging – in- Publication Data has been applied for.

PRINTED IN THE UNITED STATES OF AMERICA.

DEDICATION

This book is dedicated to my late grandfather,
Lasie Jones, Sr.

I know you are in heaven and are so proud of me. I want to thank you for all the teachings and wisdom you poured into me. I appreciate you for sharing all of your military memories with me and even your not so good life experiences. I remember the days just riding in the back of your truck or spending time with you on the front porch. The family misses you very much, but I know you are at peace with our heavenly father. You always said these words to me, "Yolanda, learn from my life and let it push you to be better." I strive to be a better version of myself every chance I get. Grandpa, I will continue to carry you in my heart and make you proud. I love you and miss you dearly!

Love your granddaughter,
Dr. Yolanda Jerry

ACKNOWLEDGEMENTS

I thank God for giving me the vision and courage to step out on faith to bring this anthology to life with the men this time. Lord, you have been my source of strength my entire life, and I am grateful. May you get all the glory because, without you, there would be no me!

To my mother, Rumualda Jones, I thank you for always supporting me and showing me what strength looks like. Besides dad, you have been my biggest supporter, nurturer and I am blessed to be your daughter. I love you!

To my daughter, Imari Smith, you are God's gift to me. You are the reason why I continue to live and work hard each day. Thank you for your unconditional love and believing in me. Always remember, I'm very proud of you and love you!

To my partner, Pastor Frank Henderson, thank you for writing the foreword. Also, thank you for your love, constant support, your wisdom, and most of all, keeping our partnership always covered in prayer. I value all you've done and will continue to do. I thank God for you and love you very much!

To the MY WALK PAST HELL VOL II: THE MEN contributing authors, the editor (TamikaINK.com), the book cover design artist (T.M. Creative), my website/graphics design artist (GeauxFig.com), family and friends who played a role in this anthology journey, I truly thank you for the love, support, trust, integrity, and commitment along the way. May God bless each one of you!

TABLE OF CONTENTS

A Message From
The Visionary Author
Dr. Yolanda Jerry

When you think of the title *MY WALK PAST HELL*, what do you think about? Let us look at the word *HELL* itself. In religion, *HELL* is an afterlife location where evil souls are subjected to punitive suffering, often torture, as eternal punishment after death. Well, truth be told, many people experience hell on earth. As a survivor of domestic violence and sexual assault, I have had to walk past hell a couple times.

If year 2020 & 2021 has taught us anything, it was that you could be either in the midst of or walking right past hell at any given moment. As stated in my visionary message from *MY WALK PAST HELL VOLUME I*, people have had obstacles, hardships, pains, traumas, or sufferings but still had to push through. *MY WALK PAST HELL VOL II: THE MEN* anthology shares compelling stories of what hell looked like through the lives of stout-hearted kings preserved by God's grace and kept alive to share their truth with the world.

I have served alongside some of these men and mentored a few, and for some of them, it is their first time meeting me. These accomplished men are GENUINE and TRANSPARENT. Their stories are very REVEALING and heart-felt. Listen...the men are

1

bringing a whole new EMPOWERING energy in year 2022 and beyond to be an example for others to follow.

As a woman who advocates for men and women who suffer in silence, I encourage you to decide you will no longer be held in bondage. Now is your time to walk past hell. Begin your healing journey today. Seek God in prayer and reach out to others to help you along the way. NO MORE SUFFERING IN SILENCE. Your MY WALK PAST HELL journey with us begins now. I hope you enjoy reading the stories in this book. Many of them are sharing their stories for the first time. Thank you for joining us on this journey. Love and blessings to you!!!

Your Visionary Author
Dr. Yolanda Jerry
www.iamyolandajerry.com

About
Dr. Yolanda Jerry

A dvocacy is centered at the heart of every Philanthropist. Echoing that notion at its finest; is the diversified professional, Dr. Yolanda Jerry. Dr. Yolanda Jerry is an International Best-Selling Author, speaker, business guru, and CEO and Founder of YJ Empowerment Solutions LLC and YJ Inspires, a multidisciplinary advocacy program, invented to help clients push beyond their past traumas and elevate to the next level, both personally and professionally. Affectionately known as the "Empowerment Advocate,"

Dr. Jerry is reputed for her innate ability to exhort multi-generational audiences through her powerful and relatable messages, as she passionately advocates for truth, healing, resiliency, and personal growth. Yolanda delivers an awe-inspiring proponent perspective against domestic violence, youth bullying, and sexual assault. Through the vernacular of a survivor, she impacts many, inspiring them to create the best version of themselves; despite tragedy, and to become intentional in the pursuit of their life's purpose and goals.

Yolanda's mantra is simple: Accept the past. Focus on the now. Impact the future.

Adding to her philanthropic capacity, Dr. Yolanda Jerry is also a retired Air Force veteran and Co-Founder of Bridging The Gap Transitional Age Youth Program. As a highly respected member of both local and national communities, Yolanda has been featured and headlined in well-respected publications, such as: the Huffington Post, Sheen Magazine, Glambitious Magazine, Courageous Woman Magazine, MizCEO Entrepreneurial Magazine, Gulf Coast Woman Magazine, Success Women's Magazine, VIP Global Magazine and many more; all highlighting the remarkable impression Yolanda has left on an ever changing world. One of Yolanda's most notable features was her article called "The Day I Decided to Leave." A compelling survivor's testament so impressive, it was chosen by highly respected, serial producer and screenwriter, Shonda Rhimes, to be displayed in her online storytelling periodical column, "Shondaland," in 2020.

Dr. Jerry is also recognized as both a highly decorated professional and nonprofit organizer, receiving numerous awards and recognition for her contributions to charity, business, military service, and community. She is the proud recipient of the Humanitarian Service Award: Trinity International University of Ambassadors, the Rising Star Award: Mississippi Gulf Coast Black Owned Businesses, "You Are Beautiful" Survivor Award & State of Connecticut Official Citation, One Coast Community Leader Award Finalist: Mississippi Gulf Coast Chamber of Commerce, Top 50 Black Women in Business in Mississippi: Black Women's Business Expo, Volunteer of the Year and Top Influencer Award: Success Women's Conference, Kish Magazine Women of Dignity Top 31 History Makers, Lifetime Achievement Award from President Biden and Vice-President Kamala Harris and many more. Yolanda currently holds chair or seat on over 14 well-respected community organizations, attesting candidly to the force she is in the arenas of business and servant leadership.

When Dr. Yolanda Jerry is not out advocating for those in need. She is a loving partner, mother, and friend.

Dr. Yolanda Jerry. Leader. Energizer. Advocate.
Connect with Dr. Yolanda Jerry
Website: www.iamyolandajerry.com
E-mail: yolanda@yjempowers.com

Foreword By Pastor Frank Henderson

If you're reading this book, God brought you here. When I was a kid, I paid more attention than I thought I did. It's amazing how much we sponge as a child simply growing up in our households and communities. One of the things that I vividly remember is my grandfather. He wasn't really in my life. I don't remember much conversation between us. I just remember that he didn't talk much. He didn't say a lot. He was a quiet man. One of the things I remember as a kid is thinking to myself concerning him, "Why didn't you tell your son to treat my mama right?"

See, I believe that silence is a form of consent and that until men begin to raise their voices in the earth again, people will simply believe that we have no qualms with anything that is going on in life, politics, religion, relationships, parenting, sex, money and more...

In barbershops all across the world, men talk. They're loud and adamant about everything. I guess we feel that the barbershop is a safe place to express ourselves. I think that's cool, but after we leave those barbershops, we need to keep talking about our lives, journeys, experiences, wins, and losses. We mustn't be silent like my grandfather. We must begin to speak in powerful ways to all of those that are coming behind us.

Dr. Yolanda Jerry has given us a "barbershop" in the form of a book. This safe space is built to give the world a glimpse into the hearts and minds of men. In this book, you'll hear of our joys and the things that have crippled us in ways that we never told a soul about.

I resolved as a young man seeing my grandfather be silent that I never would. Guess what, though? Life got me too. I stopped talking. I let conversations and attitudes slide. I took about a decade off in life. Multiple divorces had crippled my confidence and left me shivering in the cold reality of my shortcomings. One of the things that I had to learn is that without conversation, testimony, or "heart-to-heart" moments, nothing will ever change. EVER!!!!! In the garden of Eden, God talked. In creating the world, God talked. Concerning the coming of a Messiah, God talked. God is a talker, a conversationalist that wants to be intimate and speak to and with us. We are all like that because we were built in his image. The sad part is that everyone has gotten that memo, but men.

Have you ever seen in real life where you visit big mamas and everybody is talking, but granddaddy? He's on the porch cracking peanuts or tinkering with something in the garage while everyone else talks about a billion things. I wanted my grandfather to talk, I don't think others did. He was minimized, emasculated, and seen as inefficient in conversation.

My Walk Past Hell Vol II: The Men is about to change the game. People are now going to know that men have been through incredibly painful things, recognized it, and gotten better by making choices daily to walk by faith and not our own limited sight. Dr. Jerry, thanks for this "literary barbershop where men can begin to speak on it with full transparency. I can't wait to read these incredible stories.

Lastly, being asked to write this foreword is an honor. I feel as if I'm "John The Baptist" announcing the coming of Christ, except it's these incredible authors in this "My Walk Past Hell Vol II: The Men" anthology. Let me prophesy that so many men will find the courage through this book to speak out and own their lives. Many will reclaim strength. Many will visit a therapist for the first time ever. Many will talk to their kids, wives, and parents honestly like never before. Why? Because these men chose to simply be a VOICE for God and all that's good in the earth...

To every reader, open your heart and read this with it. Men are talking. Are you listening?

Frank Henderson, Lead Pastor
EPIC Fellowship Church
Rocky Mount, NC
www.epicfc.org

About
Pastor Frank Henderson

F rank Henderson is a man of many talents and skills. Raised in Rocky Mount, NC, he was heavily influenced by the leaders of his city and allowed to hone his singing and preaching skills there under the leadership of Bishop R.T. McCarter and the Morning Star Church of Christ family.

Growing up without a father figure in the home was extremely hard on him. Because of it, he developed a steely resolve to always count on himself in every situation. At the age of 15 in the summer of 82' Frank gave his life to Christ, and it began a journey of self-discovery as he began to be awakened to the things he was born to do from heaven's point of view.

Starting out as a songwriter and singer, Frank began to figure out exactly more about why he was put here on this earth. Ultimately it all led to him becoming a church planter. Over the last 20 years, Frank has planted churches in cities across North Carolina. He is currently the lead pastor at EPIC Fellowship Church, where empowering people in Christ is the only agenda.

Frank has always been bi-vocational and supported himself and his family through his work as a financial professional with some of the leading financial companies in America.

Connect with Pastor Frank Henderson

Church Website: www.epicfc.org
Frank Henderson Financial
website: www.frankhendersonfinancial.com

Shattering The Glass Ceiling
By Bishop Carl E. Jones, Sr.

Systemic Racism is nothing new; no systemic racism has been around for many years, if not decades, if not centuries. It's just that it has been often cloaked in the fabric of the United States flag as "Life, liberty and the pursuit of happiness." Whether you are in a grocery store line, buying a new car or home, or interviewing for a new job, we can see the "R" word raise its ugly head. It doesn't matter whether you are blue collar, white collar, or no collar working in these united states from main street to wall street; you could and would, in most cases, run head on into the glass ceiling that's designed to keep you in your place. For many years, I've worked in corporate America, and as I was working with one of the fortune 500 companies, I found that it isn't the fortune 500 companies that are racist, but many of the people working there that are.

As I slowly moved up the corporate ladder, I noticed that if you didn't learn the game and understand where the stones in the streams were, you could easily become the target of someone's hateful drive and motivation and have your dreams drowned because of someone's dislike for the pigmentation of your skin, the coarseness of your hair or just because of what you represented historically. It all started with wishful thinking, aspirations, plans, and dreams of what could be. I had hired on with this company, and after going through a training process in Lansing, Michigan, I was sent to the Charlotte Zone in North Carolina.

I was a member of the Charlotte Zone living in Winston Salem, North Carolina. I was the district service manager working and calling on dealers in and around the Winston-Salem area. Each year that I worked here, I could feel myself progressing and learning more about the company and its culture each day. I worked for a no non-sense ex-marine who expected you to come to work and do your job day in and day out. He was firm but fair, and with every review under his tutelage, I learned to respect him with each day because what he insisted on, he also gave, which was "Respect."

In 1987, I remembered walking into his office and asking why he looked so down and depressed? He replied we lost the aftersales service contest by 4 points. I looked him square in the eyes and let him know that we would never lose again. In 1988 not only did we win the contest, but it was a trip to Hong Kong, China, for ten days. For four years, I had matriculated and grown in the job and in my role to the point that all my reviews were graded as excellent and superior.

In 1989, I was transferred from Charlotte, North Carolina, to Dallas, Texas, where I had been told that I would be the metro district service manager. To my dismay and chagrin, I met with my new assistant manager-service and was told that I would not be taking over the Dallas metro district but that I would be covering West Texas, which included Los Cruces, New

Mexico, instead. This assignment guaranteed that I would be on the road at least 3 to 4 nights per week in this district.

I had been there approximately one month when I was called into his office and told he was not satisfied with the job I was doing, and if I didn't pick up the pace, my behavior would be reflected in my annual reviews. Now mind you, I had worked for an ex-marine who was my supervisor at the time for four years in Charlotte and had never received less than excellent or superior on any annual reviews working for this company. So, in my mind, I'm thinking, "what changed, what was different?" I had worked there for six months, and as a young father with a newborn baby boy at home, I was away from home more than I was home.

On the day of my review, I prayed before going into the office; I noticed my supervisor made me wait for three hours before he met with me. He kept going into and out of the Zone Managers' office with what I felt was my review in his hands. We finally met, and it was clear that he was flustered and seemed to be upset about something and he proceeded to go over my review and tell me that my work was less than satisfactory. During our discussion, everything I said or asked was met with resentment and disdain for reasons I didn't understand at the time. On my review, I was given a job performance rating "unsatisfactory", which I questioned and was basically told to be glad that I still had a job.

Even with this review that was clearly subjective, I asked the question, "How is it that I had received *excellent & superior* scores coming out of Charlotte but was now being put on an Employee Improvement Plan six months later?"

This review was filled with lies and made-up situations that were clearly designed to malign my name and ultimately cost me my job. I also asked when I could be considered for a district manager sales position, and with his face red as a beet, he stated emphatically that this would never happen on his watch. I stated I didn't understand why, and he stated I needed to talk to the zone manager. I asked for an audience, which never happened. After being told I would never be on the sales side of the business, I had to realize that this was white collar racism right before my very eyes. The heat only got hotter with this man calling me day in and day out, calling me in dealerships before 8 a.m. and many times after 5 p.m.

For the next two years, I was subjected to ridicule, blame, and all sorts for clandestine activities that were clearly designed to make me quit or give up. My expense reports were scrutinized and checked weekly, and charges were denied, all with the support of the Zone Manager. I talked with my dad, and he said, "If I didn't teach ya'll boys anything else, I taught you once you start something, you better not quit and don't allow someone to make you quit."

With that being said, I recognized that I knew something that my racist supervisor didn't know; I knew that if I held my peace and let the Lord fight this battle, victory would be mine. This is where I'm so thankful to the Pastor and my Sunday School Teachers, who had taught me to have faith even when it didn't make sense because with God, "No weapon formed against me would prosper and every tongue that rises against me God would condemn."

Can you say the heat got hotter? Little did I know that the enemy was turning up the heat through this man who was my supervisor even more. I called my father, and once again, he told him what I was up against and that I was considering quitting the company. My dad asked me, "Carl are you doing your best?"

To which I answered, "Yes, Sir!"

He said, "Listen, son in life, you will encounter all sorts of people who will lie, cheat and steal and drag your name through the dirt, but the one thing I know is this...if it's a lie, it will die, and the Lord has got his hands on you. You just continue to do your job and don't allow no man to shake your faith."

Over the next year, I knew what I was fighting against, and it wasn't just a demon in the flesh but principalities, powers, and spiritual wickedness in high places. My family and I started attending First Baptist Church, Dallas, Texas, where I realized that God was up to something. Because after attending for about three to four Sundays, we joined, and the Pastor said, "Where have you been? I've been waiting on you."

This was when I discovered that the glass ceiling above my head was not the result of the company but many of the people working in the company. However, this is also when God revealed to me that "what He (God) has for you is for you." The yearly and by-yearly reviews were all the same stamped "unsatisfactory."

They caught the attention of the HR department, who reached out to my previous supervisor in Charlotte, who let them know without question that while working for him, I had been a superior employee and that he would recommend me for the district manager sales job.

My old supervisor from Charlotte then called me and said to me, "If you can outlive a bad or erroneous review, you can outlive a bad manager, stay focused." The conversation we had added to the fire already burning inside of me, and I was determined to shatter the glass ceiling especially knowing that I was a child of the most high God. I knew that *I could do all things through Christ who strengthens me and that all things work together for their good of those who love the Lord and are called according to his purposes.*

You see, systemic racism and Injustices are often hidden behind the curtains of what usually is really happening in the workplace. Listen, workplace racism and injustice are no joke when we look at the lives of Alton Sterling, Philando Castille, Tamir Rice, Sandra Bland, Eric Garner, Ahmad Aubery, and George Floyd's deaths at the hands of white police officers and citizens who are taking the law into their own hands because they felt entitled to do so. But if you will notice protests, systemic racism, and injustice have geared up across the country, now it's prompting companies and citizens alike to speak out in support of racial justice. They're sharing lengthy statements declaring "black lives matter" to staff and the public, pledging millions to social justice organizations, and even marking

Juneteenth as a company holiday. The leadership in a lot of these fortune 500 companies are apologizing and resigning over problematic company culture, where diversity was spoken but not realized or recognized.

Systemic racism and Injustice within the workplace won't be resolved in one news cycle, one newspaper article, webinar, or zoom call. If the truth be known, over half of the black employees in these United States have felt racism and injustice in the workplace and society. One study shows that only 3.2% of executives and senior manager–level employees are black, and only five *Fortune* 500 CEOs are. According to another study, black men are paid 13% less than white men; black women are paid 39% less than white men and 21% less than white women. They ask for promotions and raises at about the same rate as white women but get worse results. Martin Luther King said, "Injustice anywhere is a threat to justice everywhere."

So back to my walk past my hell and how God brought me out. This supervisor continued his antics, harassment, and outright racism, and as I stated earlier, the HR department got involved and began an investigation. While they never gave me the results of their investigation, in October 1992, I transferred to the Pittsburgh Zone in Pittsburgh, Pennsylvania, where unlike the four-year nightmare I had just lived through. The Assistant Zone Manager – Service contacted me, and he stated that because the Zone Team was heading for an offsite meeting in a nearby city, and the Zone Manager would be picking me up. I was floored because after living through the pure hell of the Dallas Area, the Pittsburgh Zone Manager was picking me up, and he would bring me to the Golf Resort where the meeting was taking place.

I was not only thanking God for bringing me through, but He had also allowed me to see that red-eyed racism of some was not the order of the day for all. On the Monday of the next week, I was called into the office to meet with the Zone Manager, and you've got to know that I had my guard up because I wasn't sure what to expect. I sat in my car and prayed for 15 minutes asking the Lord to go before me.

When I entered his office, he and the assistant manager – service were sitting there, and we exchanged salutations, with respect, and professionalism and almost simultaneously they both stated that from this point forward, I was to call them by their first names. The Zone Manager then asked me if I knew why I was transferred to the Pittsburgh Area. I replied, "I have some idea, but I wasn't sure you would share it with me."

He stated, "You damn right I'm going to share it with you."

He made a phone call, and to my dismay, as I listened, I realized that he was talking to the VP of Sales and Marketing from the home office; but I heard him say, "These reviews that I'm reading about Carl Jones are total BS, and I want them taken out of his record." He further stated that "With the experience, Mr. Jones has both retail and wholesale, he would be the perfect fit to pilot the new Combo District Sales and Service Managers position."

I could not believe my ears; Lord, am I hearing him correctly? Did he just say what I thought he said? After a lengthy conversation with the VP, he hung up the phone, and his administrative assistant walked in and said HR was on the line. The Zone Manager put it on speaker because they obviously wanted me to hear what was transpiring. The HR Manager stated that the zone manager's request to throw out the last four years of my reviews from the previous area had been granted, and the assistant zone manager – service of the prior site, had been forced to retire.

I excused myself and went to my car, and began to thank God for all that he was doing in my life at this moment. So not only did I become a District Sales Manager, but I spent the next fourteen years with the company climbing the corporate ladder. My last position was that of Zone Manager for a major division within the company in the Pittsburgh Area. I was selected Zone Manager of the year in 2006, 2007, and 2008. During my time with the company, God had called me to the ministry, and I became Pastor of Greater Parkview Church in July 2003. God had shown me over the many years that when I didn't think he was there, he always was. He had proven to me that my faith had opened the doors and caused me to endure the struggles and the fires of the hell I had come through. Listen, there are many things in this life we can't count on, but all I can tell you is with God, ALL things are possible. Through shattering the glass ceiling, God had also shown me that there's no success without a struggle, and there's no testimony without a test. With my walk past hell, I want to encourage somebody reading this who's ready to throw in the towel, who's feeling down and depressed, not to give up. Don't ever give up! Yes, your plans might seem to be poisoned, your aspirations might seem to have been aborted, your dreams might look like they are drowning, but if you look to the hills from which comes all our help, you will see that our God can do anything but fail. Just as God was with David, Elijah, Paul, and Carl, He will also take care of you.

About
Bishop Carl E. Jones, Sr.

B ishop Carl E. Jones, Sr., has served as the pastor of Greater Parkview Church (GPC) in Greensburg, PA, since July 2003. He began his Christian walk at an early age, where he accepted Christ and was baptized. He served in various ministries from his youth and through his adulthood. He credits a lot of Greater Parkview's excellence to God and his ministry mentor and father, Bishop Leslie Patterson, Pastor, First Baptist Church of Sterling, VA, who continues to be a great source of leadership and guidance. In March 2009, Pastor Jones and the members of GPC purchased the new and current church edifice. He has pastored Greater Parkview Church for the past 18 years.

Bishop Jones is bi-vocational and holds a BA Degree in Business/Marketing from Northwood University. He was a Middle Management Executive employed by General Motors for 20 years and has spent the last five years with Nissan North America. He is currently completing his studies to obtain his Masters of Divinity (MDiv)Degree through United Theological Seminary.

Bishop Jones is a member and former Branch President of the Greensburg-Jeannette NAACP. He has a partner in ministry, his wife Stephanie, and three children: Carl, Jr., Forrest, and Olivia. He is dedicated to his family, church family, his relatives, and friends. His life is indicative of his favorite words, "People don't care how much you know UNTIL they know how much you care."

Connect with Bishop Jones. Sr and his ministry
Website: www.greaterparkviewchurch.net

To Hell and Back Again!
By Lee A. Wright

Why is it that when your mother and father came together sexually (consensually or otherwise), out of approximately 5000 sperm, you were the one that reached and penetrated the egg in your mother's womb? That's a 1 in 5000 chance!!! What if I told you that in spite of what you may have heard in your life, that you are not here by mistake? What if I told you that God has plans for your life? What if from the time you were born, you were chosen and set apart for a purpose? That through your life, it would impact thousands of people, and yet you may never reach "celebrity status?" What if I told you that you may never get to the point in life where your signature becomes an autograph? What if I told you that in your lifetime, you'd literally have to go through Hell? What would you do?

Hell is a very real place! We as human beings sometimes forget that Hell can also be a situation that you are going through. Or, as I like to say, a situation that you are _"growing" through_. A little-known preacher once said that if you learn to **_grow through_** instead of just **_go through_**, that you won't have to keep **_going through_** the same thing over and over again. Who would ever imagine that men go through Hell just as much as women do? And just like women, we as men don't talk about it. We keep it bottled up inside, and unfortunately, when it comes out, it can be in an unhealthy manner. It's time that I begin to lift the veil!

Imagine being a young man with an urge to serve your country. I enlisted in the United States Air Force, wanting to do something different from the normal. I knew that service would provide an exit from living in my small town. However, I also knew that with service, there's the possibility that I may have to lay down my life in service to the country. Because my father had served in the United States Marine Corps during the Vietnam War, he would share stories about losing close friends. Since we weren't "at war," I assumed that that wouldn't even come into play. Boy, was I in for a wakeup call?

In March of 1996, I was deployed to Dharan, Saudi Arabia, with my unit. We were doing our "annual" rotation. We would routinely deploy during Christmas, but this time we got the spring/summer rotation. Scorching hot days! Followed up by mild 98-degree nights! It seemed like business as usual. That is until the evening of June 25, 1996. A terrorist group decided to detonate a truck bomb outside of my housing complex. Nineteen American Airmen lost their lives that night in the attack, and hundreds more were injured. I was one of the injured, and of the nineteen, twelve were friends/co-workers of mine. For perspective, imagine yourself in a room with nineteen other people. Twelve of them, you know, and seven you don't. Close your eyes and open them. Now you're the only one in the room, and you'll never see them again! I was 24 years old at the time, and my world was just turned upside down! I'd survived, but now what do I do? Do I finish my enlistment and go back to my hometown? Do I continue to serve my country knowing this had just happened? In a sort of crazy twist of fate, my decision was made for me less than one month later. You see, after my deployment, my intentions were to go to Atlanta, Georgia, for a little R&R (Rest & Relaxation).

The 1996 Olympic Games were happening there, and how often does a person get to see the Olympic Games in person? However, due to the bombing, I had just experienced, I decided to stay close to home. As many people know, a bomb was also set off in the Olympic Park that summer. My thoughts immediately turned to what I had just experienced! More importantly, I thought to myself, "that could have been me. I was supposed to be there!" Those two incidents would guide my life for years to come. I decided to continue in military service because I told myself it doesn't matter whether I'm a civilian or military. If it's my time, it's my time! God is in control! Through this storm, it was difficult for me to deploy again, and yet I did by trusting God. After twenty-six years of service, I retired from the Air Force. The scars remain, but I'm a survivor!

Life has a funny way of teaching you lessons...if you're willing to learn them. Five years after the attack, I'd found the love of my life. The person I was supposed to spend the rest of my life with...or so I thought. Through our union, we brought a beautiful baby girl into this world. In this relationship, we definitely had our share of ups and downs. We weren't the Cosby's, but I didn't think things were that bad either. I came from a broken home and watched my father abuse my mother. Watching her run out of the house and down the street while being chased by my dad with a BB rifle that he'd purchased for me...it leaves an image! I'd always told myself that when I was married, I'd never do the things my father did. We all come with baggage and scars! If you don't take time to deal with your past hurt, it can affect your future in a negative way.

Counseling is such a "taboo" word, especially in the African-American community. I would venture to say that if she and I had taken the time to get counseling in dealing with our issues, things might have turned out differently. I'm not just talking about pre-marital counseling; I'm referring to life counseling in general. Being raised in a single-parent home will develop you differently than a two-parent household, not necessarily in a negative way, just different. At the time, I didn't really understand or even know how to deal with past traumas and hurts within myself or my spouse.

In my mind, I had this image of a fairytale marriage where we never argued or had issues. Unfortunately, that wasn't very realistic. Because neither one of us took time to deal with past hurts from relationships or upbringing, and it found its way into our home.

Over time, the relationship began to erode. We argued over things which today, I can't even remember what they were about. What I do remember is the moment I snapped. It was early morning; I was about to head to work, and we had another argument. I walked out of the front door angrily, and my wife slammed the door behind me! That slammed door triggered a response that I was not prepared for. I turned back toward the door and literally kicked it so hard it came off the hinges! When I saw what I had done, I paused for a moment to process everything, then left to go to work. I went straight into the office of my leadership (First Sergeant) to explain what had just happened. After all, I'm in the military, so it's about to come to light. Repair to the door and repayment was obvious. But I now had to deal with something much deeper.

I knew I had just become my father! No, I didn't physically put my hands on her, but the fact I was able to do what I did...my reaction to this external stimulus was a sign that this relationship had to end. In our past arguments, we would both talk about divorce; however, we'd always talk through it and find our footing again. This is a hard lesson to deal with coming from a person who is supposed to live their life by a certain standard. These are not the actions of a man! These are not the actions of a husband! These are not the actions of a Christian!

We eventually divorced, and, in my haste, to be away from my wife, I represented myself in court. You know what they say about those who represent themselves. I gave her whatever she wanted just to be away from her. The worst part was that I didn't fight to have a larger part of my daughter's life! The scars were deep and remain, but I'm a survivor!

Second time around love? Is it really possible? It has to be because eight or nine years later, I gave marriage another chance. From this union sprang two children. This time a girl and a boy! I can honestly say that things in this marriage were a lot different from my first marriage. I was determined to make it work this time. After all, we learn from our past mistakes, so we don't repeat them, right? Well, I did learn. My "daddy issues" didn't come popping up. But that doesn't mean there weren't new issues and challenges to deal with. There's a lot to be said for communication. It's a two-way street and when the communication stops, so does the relationship. I worked hard to provide for my family, working a full-time job and two side gigs to make ends meet. I'm not here to slam to the mother(s) of my children. I don't do it in front of the children, and I won't do it in a book.

I won't allow the issues we had to affect the relationship between a mother and her children. My mother never bad mouthed my father to me! I had my own type of relationship with him based on our interactions, not theirs! I will say for those that are single, married, divorced, and anywhere in between, you have to communicate and learn the good and not so good with your partner. You have to talk about your likes and dislikes—children, finances, education, your past relationships, as well as the goals you have in life. If you dig deep enough to gain understanding, I believe many pitfalls are avoidable.

Mistrust, fabricated lies, infidelity, broken boundaries, a lack of accountability and enabling. I don't introduce these terms lightly. These are some of the things I experienced during my two marriages. Hard life lessons to have to deal with at any age.

The thing I knew this time as divorce came rearing its head...I was going to fight for my children! Fight to be in their lives and not give up! Men, hear me on this one! If you are doing everything you can possibly do as a husband/father and things still don't work out, don't be afraid to fight for your children. Long gone are the days when custody is awarded "automatically" to the mother. I fought for custody of my children this time. I fought for the right to be the primary provider! There are far too many absentee fathers in this world! My father, for many years of my adult life, was one.

I say that because even as "adults," we still need our parents help to guide, shape, and mold us. I read a quote one day from an unknown author that said, "one thing that we don't realize while we're growing up is that our parents are still growing up too." I can admit to you that after my first divorce, I became an absentee father too. Sure, I provided my monthly child support payments faithfully until my daughter graduated High School. But the other areas of love, nurturing, spending time with my daughter, I was woefully lacking! It's not that I couldn't do, it's that I didn't do that! I have to live with that! I have to own that! And I do! Because of that, I was determined to fight this time! After weighing everything, the court ruled in my favor, and I was awarded primary custody of our two children. And no,

I didn't represent myself this time! The scars were deep and remain, but I'm a survivor!

Trust me when I tell you it's not easy. So, to all the single dads out there that are holding it down for your children, I salute you! Because if I'm being 100% transparent, when it came to my first daughter, I wasn't there like a father should be. Again, I have to live with that! I have to own it! At the time of this printing, she's a college student and doing extremely well. I can't take any credit for it, but I will give kudos to her mother. She did a fantastic job, and though we didn't make it, she raised a phenomenal young lady.

And though wife number two for me didn't work out, we are learning to co-parent very well – something that was lacking with wife number one. Guess what? It's not about you, and it's not about her. It's about these precious lives that you have created, and God has entrusted to your care.

Through the relationships not working out, I've learned not only to make sure my children are taken care of in more areas than just financial but to take care of me. I take time for me. I get away. A day trip, a weekend away; Building things that have added value to my home. If I allowed my failed marriages to affect me negatively, I wouldn't be able to care for myself or my children. You may get down, but don't stay down. The bible says, "let us not be weary in well doing; for in due season we shall reap, if we faint not." (Gal 6:9) In this last divorce, I lost a lot of stuff. But the stuff I lost was material. It hurt to lose my stuff, but you know what? I went out and bought new stuff. I saved up for the things I wanted and needed. I don't owe the furniture company; I don't owe Uncle Mastercard and Aunt Visa! I don't owe the IRS! He whom the Son sets free, is free indeed!

I got to the point in life where I could spend a week with my children at Disney World, as expensive as it is down there, and not blink an eye because everything we did was already paid for before we arrived or I had the finances to get while we were there! That's freedom! To have the company you work for make a payroll error, forget to pay you, and you can still pay your utility bills, that's freedom!

To every man that reads this book and reads this chapter, I need to tell you this...it's not going to be easy, but I can tell you that it's going to be worth it! Get up, dust yourself off and start over again. If you're going to LEVEL UP, you've got to first LEVEL! If you've ever played a video game in your youth, you know that there are levels in the game. You can't move to the next level without completing the level that you're on. And if the game wins, do you put it up and never play again? God forbid. You know how to hit the reset button and get back in the game! You wore out the PS1 and graduated to a PS2! Some of you may even be on the PS5! My point is that life will take you through some obstacles and changes. Don't give up on life! Don't stop believing that God still has a plan for you!

Jesus met a woman at a well, and He asked her where her husband was; she told him she didn't have one. He said, you're right, you've had five of them! And the one you're with now is not your husband! With all of her issues, Jesus still used her to convert an entire city!

Don't let your past "fails" make you think you're a failure! Shake it off! Don't give up on your goals and dreams! If God is in it, it will happen. "I'll never save $100!" Start with saving $1 and do it 100 times! "I'll never save $1000" Start with saving $100 and do it 10 times! "I'll never be able to find a wife!" Start with seeing yourself as a husband!

So, when you see me smiling despite what I've been through, it's because I'm still here! I haven't given up on life, and amazingly, I haven't given up on love. In the business world, I wear many hats. I still work for the Department of Defense; I'm an author, speaker, minister, comedian, mentor, DJ, father, son, and friend! I have three amazing children who love me as much as I love them! We have food, shelter, and clothing. I'm extremely blessed! While the world almost came to a complete halt due to a global pandemic, I've been busy building something that my future self will be thankful for. If at the end of this journey I'm on, I can hear the words, "This is my beloved son in whom I'm well pleased," my work will be complete. We all experience a type of Hell in our lives. Mental, physical, emotional, and even spiritual. And yes, there can be multiple occurrences. We learn from our personal experiences, and I pray that you can also learn not only from mine, but the other phenomenal men sharing their truths.

I stand by this mantra in life. "I am NOT a product of my circumstances; I'm a product of my decisions." I can't blame what I'm growing through or have grown through on my mom or dad...my ex-wives...where I grew up, or what I didn't have. At the end of the day, the one person that I have the most control over is myself, my actions, my inactions, my reactions. IT'S TIME! You decide what you are going to be!!! You decide to be a survivor!!! You are the head and not the tail!!! You decide to take your walk PAST Hell!!!

About
Lee A. Wright

Motivation is centered at the heart of every Mentor. Echoing that notion at its finest; is the diversified professional, Mr. Lee A. Wright.

Mr. Lee A. Wright is a Combat Wounded Terrorist Attack Survivor, speaker, businessman, and CEO and Founder of Lee A Wright Solutions, LLC and Legit One Productions, LLC, a multidisciplinary speaking and entertainment company with motivational speakers, DJ's and comedian's, created to help clients find laughter in joyful as well as difficult times, push beyond their past hurt and pain, and elevate to the next level, both personally and professionally. Along the way music was brought under the umbrella because it is soothing to the soul. Affectionately known as "Doc", Mr. Wright is reputed for his innate ability to exhort multi-generational audiences through his powerful, relevant, and relatable messages on truth, healing, finance and empowering personal growth.

Mr. Lee A. Wright hails from Boynton Beach, FL and entered the Air Force in November of 1989 and retired in December of 2015. He has three children, Kaila, Kaydence and Kolton. In his 26-year Air Force career, he held many challenging leadership positions to include serving as a Technical Training instructor, serving as an Air Force First Sergeant, and serving on the Air Education & Training Command Inspector General team. He deployed numerous times, supporting various operations to include OPERATION Southern Watch.

Lee's Mantra: "I am NOT a product of my circumstances. I am a product of my decisions."
When Lee A. Wright is not out speaking and mentoring those in need. He is a devoted son, father, and friend.

Connect with Lee Wright
E-mail: mrleeawright@gmail.com
Website: https://www.iamleeawright.com

The Perfect Problem
By C. Richaude Dorsey

The year was 1987 when I was initially introduced into my battle with addiction. I was ten years old with hopes of turning 11 in a few months as every child wishes for. Little did I know that there was a detour that the enemy placed into my pathway on my way home from school one day when I was in the 5th grade. I was introduced to a whole new world that I had no clue would expose me to a set of challenges designed to place me out of the will of my God-given purpose of empowering others.

As a child in the third grade, I was diagnosed with Attention Deficit Hyperactivity Disorder (ADHD) and an additional diagnosis that shall remain nameless. At the age of nine, I was tremendously impacted by the medication I was placed under to alleviate the issues that came along with this condition. As time progressed over the years, I began to experience the problems associated with being heavily medicated in order to get through a "said" normal day. From early childhood into adolescence, I was always viewed as an individual with an outgoing personality with a fond love for music which explained the reason behind me being formally trained from an early age in piano as well as drums.

Throughout the years of dealing with mind-altering medication, this began to adversely impact my personality in multiple ways. I began to struggle with social acceptance from peers and family members, which in time placed me on the road to dealing with depression. I had become withdrawn from others unless my love for the arts and public speaking was involved. I absolutely hated the fact that I was viewed as being "different" by most of the social circles that I was around. With time I began to use drugs to mask the challenges that came along with not being socially accepted due to the problems accompanied by my condition. Coupled with being heavily medicated over the years and being introduced to a newly found "friend," a chemical imbalance had been created, which created a total personality difference in me. I had no idea that my actions were detrimental to my mental health because I was so young. Furthermore, I had no idea that I had a predisposition to addiction because of my family history (read between the lines). This was not revealed until later.

I grew up in a wonderful home with two parents that provided an amazing life for my siblings and me. We had our fair share of issues, as any family does. We faced problems that most would not have believed had we not told them (AND NO, THE LIGHTS DIDN'T GET CUT OFF! LOL). This taught me into adulthood that an individual can come from the ideal situation or environment as I did but still battle internal issues that can, at some point, bring one to a breaking point with time. I can vividly remember the fond memories of my mother providing me with daily positive affirmations in order to warrant success in the lives of my siblings and me. My father was a hard worker, and my mother was as well. Both parents did exceptionally well within their crafts and were diligent in gaining momentum in their careers. However, they had a child (me) that battled with the lack of acceptance in the academic environment and most social settings due to having an "active" lifestyle in most cases. Finding my niche in life, which was making others laugh and music, allowed my safe haven to be formulated, nourished, and developed.

Eventually, I was placed into therapy at an early age which I thought was supposed to assist me and my family in dealing with my internal issues. The strategies that my therapist team implemented into my life, with time, would not only provide me with a mirrored image of the "real me" but also provide me with a personal reality of how much I did not like who I was at the time. This eventually introduced me to another problem in an attempt to embellish the view that others had of me. From childhood into my adolescence, I never actually liked myself or even accepted being different. This was a false sense of reality that the enemy painted for me. Since there was a predisposition to addiction and a clinical diagnosis and emotional issues in place, this would eventually be ingredients for my downward spiral.

I began using alcohol and smoking marijuana at a very young age (elementary school). I smoked my first joint when I was in the 5th grade. As you read previously, I was already under a doctor's care due to the conditions I suffered with. As I stated earlier, our family had suppressed issues that were being dealt with from a professional standpoint. For me to deal with the struggles and stress of having to deal with it, the substance use began to numb me of the issues I experienced within the residential environment. I thought that every issue that I experienced in every aspect of my life could be forgotten about or numbed if I got high. I worried about my parents a lot as a child. They had no idea. I worried about my father because of who he was. The same applied to my mom. Whenever their issues arose, I would drink. I can vividly remember starting to drink more than most of my peers even knew into junior high school. I guess you may be asking, "How does a 13-14-year-old get drunk, and nobody notices?"

During those days, I found it relatively easy to hide it. I would often drink mouthwash to hide it or eat mustard. Yep, you read right. If you want to hide alcohol, just chase it with a spoon of mustard. If you drink vodka, nobody will smell it unless they drink OFTEN. These were tricks that I learned at an early age. Additionally, I also learned that most adults would think they were barking up the wrong tree if they even thought to accuse a teenager at CHURCH of smelling like alcohol and marijuana. So, with that being stated, I was looked over and given the benefit of the doubt.

I was raised in the church from birth under the system of religion. Although the protocol of religion was in place, there was absolutely no Godly relationship being developed internally, which meant there was no conviction of any kind being fulfilled in my life. What little conviction that was inside of me came from God himself, which I had no clue about until later on in adolescence, when I became more spiritually groomed enough to know God's voice. Here I was in junior high school living as an addict. Yes. Acceptance was a journey, and at the time, I had no clue what the issue was due to the many influences of music, society, and the lack of my personal relationship with God. I struggled with depression, self-acceptance, and lack of acceptance within the kindling of relationships (dating). I was not always the guy that girls went after, which frustrated me even more because Lord knows I always had a fond love for the opposite sex. This drove me to eventually internalize more of my issues. Imagine being a young teenager and never seeming to achieve the acceptance of the opposite sex. But, as time went on, I began to utilize my gift of music and comedic personality to achieve the results I desired to have with the opposite sex. Laughter and music coupled with substance abuse opened a gateway to many opportunities for wrongful decision making. Over the years, I developed anger issues which affected the development of meaningful relationships as well. Little did I know that most of that stemmed from addiction and my internal problems.

If you notice, in the above passage, I stated that there was a "gateway" opened. If you think about it, a gate is what you see when you arrive at someone's home or a random building. The door is what you see next. If there is no gate present, then the property is what you see (usually a yard if it's a home involved). Follow me here! Doors are usually behind the gateway. If you open the gate, then one can generally receive access to the building, which is easily accessed through the door. Selah (Hebrew term meaning "to think on these things"). What this means is that there was a gateway that opened the doors to each challenge that has negatively impacted my life. In this case, I was the gate. Lack of self-acceptance opened the door to substance abuse. Substance abuse and alcoholism opened the door to anger and promiscuity. Promiscuous thoughts opened the door to the action with the opposite sex. Sexual activity opened the door to multiple doors because I was paired with other people's problems because of the created soul ties. Soul ties! That's for another book. This all led to depression. Depression helped to foster anger. The anger stemmed from the challenges of being different and never being like everyone else. Imagine coming from a good home with a few "good boy" rules while living the life of an adult and making decisions that would one day place me under the total surrender of God himself.

Upon entering high school, I was tremendously overcome with the anxiety and anticipation of the road ahead while tackling academics, extracurricular activities, and being socially accepted as the funny guy who everyone knew commonly used drugs and alcohol. Fostering meaningful relationships had become a tasking effort. Often, I found myself shunning the very individuals who harbored my best interests. There were only two individuals who defied the enemy's plans on my life relationship-wise. Gregg Magee and Marc Lemon (RIP) were the two guys I accredit with my personal growth and progress within the Kingdom. These two guys were responsible for the positive seeds of growth and development in my life at the time. These two would often discuss Jesus Christ with me and what it meant to live a life that was Kingdom oriented, and the importance of Christ-like spiritual fulfillment. Although it would be years before I knew that these guys were God sent, it would soon be revealed what vital role they played in my life. I steadily continued to live a hellish lifestyle throughout these years from age 16-21.

Over the years, I noticed that even though I had childhood friends that I was around often, there was still something missing within my immediate circle. I was only concerned with people that used drugs, and I was secretly associating myself with individuals that used hard drugs, which eventually led me down another road. Secretly, I was introduced to pornography and pimping into early adulthood. I got involved in risky sexual behavior with the opposite sex to mask my lack of self-acceptance. Although some may foster the thought that this behavior should be deemed socially acceptable, I now know that any time there is a feeling of the need to have multiple sexual partners, there is a spiritual void that needs to be fulfilled. This period of my life came along with an additional door being opened. It came with exposure to cocaine and an addiction to opiates as well.

I began lacing my marijuana with opiates because, honestly, I tapped out of acquiring the desired feeling of just "normal drugs." By the time I got to college, I had experienced tremendous weight loss due to my substance abuse issues. I noticed that my body had truly become chemically dependent upon whatever substance I had chosen to partake of. I had begun to withdraw from activities that I had a strong love for. Music was one of them. My ability to make people laugh never subsided. Lord knows some of my best material was produced during my highest moments. Since I was high the majority of the time, music was something that I remained consistent with. The musical material that I would compose under the influence was amazing, which influenced me to use more as time went by.

The enemy made me think that I could only produce quality material if I used drugs. Don't get me wrong. The material was awesome, but I noticed later that there was a demonic undertone. Many individuals don't realize that the heart of the author always follows the music. Later on, I began to use my gift of music to seduce and manipulate women. This was actually a form of witchcraft. I did not realize that then. I was treading on dangerous territory. At the same time, I was finally being accepted amongst the ranks. I began to think that now "I am finally being accepted by chicks." Even though it was on a small scale, it actually worked. This grew tremendously as time went on.2

The seemingly good thing about my life during this time was that all of it could be easily masked as me being a "party animal." Nobody would ever suspect that I had any issues with myself if I hid behind the ability to make others laugh and use music as a means to hide behind my struggle.

My college years at Alcorn State University are memorable but, at the same time, are considerably a blur because of my addiction. I have memories but, then again, not so much (IF THAT MAKES SENSE). During those years, my mother had developed a wonderful life with God. She got saved when I was struggling the most with my addiction. I sometimes say that I think she got saved to bring me in through her prayers and through the amazing leadership she was under during that timeframe. To this day, being in my hometown and visiting other places that I frequented during those years, people often attempt to present me with memories that they said I created for them with stories that I have no concrete memory of.

I had begun to experience blackouts as a result of my alcoholism. I had no clue then, but I now know that when an individual begins to experience blackouts, it directly reflects a problematic situation. I would go through periods where I would not remember a thing that happened the day or night after. You see, addiction will have you in a world of your own even when you have people in your life that are there for you daily. I have also noticed that being an individual with a history of addiction, an addict can fool and manipulate the ones that are right under their noses. I cannot count the relationships and career opportunities lost due to poor decision-making associated with substance abuse.

Once upon a time, I can vividly remember being offered a position with a very reputable corporation that shall remain nameless to provide me with an extremely lucrative opportunity. However, I was asked to provide a urine sample. DO NOT LAUGH! Well, since I knew I would be unable to provide the desired results from the drug test, I asked a very dear friend of mine to commit to providing a urine sample, and it happened to be a female. WRONG MOVE!!! The Human Resources department contacted me after the submission of the sample. They called me and, of course, I politely answered the phone. This is how the conversation went.

Me: "Hello."
Human Resources Officer: "May I speak to Mr. Dorsey?"
Me: "Speaking."
Human Resources Officer: This is Kathy from _____. How are you today?"
Me: "Doing well and yourself?"
Human Resources Officer: "Fine. Thanks for asking. Mr. Dorsey. Are you pregnant? Because if you are, then you have defied the odds of humanity. You see, Mr. Dorsey, we do not tolerate employees who do not operate under integral principles. Your urine sample reflected that you were pregnant, which means that your urine sample was tampered with, and you provided us with a

false submission. We're sorry. Your interview was unmatched, but your urinalysis did not reflect the character that this company endorses. This means that you have been denied this employment opportunity. Have a nice day."
Me: "Have a nice day."

My world came crashing down on me at that point. I lost an opportunity that would change my trajectory within the professional sector. Although it would have caused me to cut my academic career short, it still was a very lucrative opportunity to move past the challenges I faced at the time. This was just one of many opportunities lost due to the difficulties that accompanied my addiction. Later on, I developed a relationship with God after years of drugs and alcohol. I decided that enough was enough, and after being in college off and on until age 26. Yes, 26. Here I was in an undergrad program at the age of 26 years old, still trying to "find myself." I was actually walking around in circles. An old relative of mine used to always say, "If you walk back and forth down the same street, you will pass by the same houses."

That phrase began to make sense after all the years that had flown by. I sat in my dorm room at the age of 26 and realized that I would have graduated FOUR GRADUATIONS ago. My life had fallen apart, and my parents had stopped all that they were willing to do for me any further. I had ruined meaningful relationships, and all I had to show for it was a student loan bill that had far surpassed the norm, no car, no money, and no financial aid. Let's not forget about that relationship with God that my mother had initiated within her life. It was her prayers that placed me on my knees in my dorm room on 11/12/2003 at Alcorn State University. I gave my life to Christ that evening. I called my mom and told her that I had given up on living foolishly and that I had gotten saved. What I failed to say within this chapter is that years before this moment occurred is that I had begun to visit the church with my mother periodically when I would come home.

What I didn't know was that "these people" had begun praying for me without my knowledge years before I gave my life to Christ. So, while I was struggling with my most difficult times with addiction, God had placed the Kingdom citizens on alert to pray for me and to keep me covered during that time. During those years of praying, their prayers kept me grounded. There was death all around me. Of course, it was never me, but I was close. I remember the death of a good friend happening right in the car that was in front of me on the high. During those years, a shooting occurred involving a friend that happened a second after I left. During that timeframe, there were instances that I was found passed out on car hoods at nightclubs for hours high on drugs, and I was awakened with no harm. During that time, I instructed people to live a better life only to find out that they were dead no more than a week later. There were times that I could have ended up in prison because of being associated with people who committed crimes connected to trending news stories of the day. And to think THEY ARE ALL DEAD NOW—all of them.

The people I instructed to do better, EVEN WHILE I WAS IN MY MESS, are mostly dead. Family members that I hung with that were doing the same thing I was doing. (((DEAD))) If I haven't noticed anything else, I have seen that addiction plays a vital role in decision making as well as judgment. It is important to note and remain mindful that even though an addict can be sober if they are not careful, the individual can still continue to make judgments/decisions under the mindset of addiction. I have learned that when you deal with having an addictive personality, one can tend to make hasty decisions amid chaotic situations. This can always breed conditions of a negative nature. Learning to assess any situation calmly can and will always warrant success, especially when the pros and cons can be weighed.

Attempting to live by this principle was thoroughly tested in my first marriage. With time I was tested. Your testimony will be tried by fire. Taking on too many endeavors and juggling them all was a bad move. Even though I had sobered up all of the unpacked baggage set up residence in my new life. As time progressed, I found myself heavily involved in ministry. When ministry is involved, you will find that the enemy will fight you with the demons you fought while you were in your mess. This is precisely what happened. Along with the stress of everyday life, I found myself resorting back to drugs and alcohol as a coping skill to manage my adversities. WOW! Now I'm in the church, active in ministry, married, and using drugs/alcohol. How did I end back up on this road again?

I learned during this time that an unhealed individual will soon backtrack to what is comfortable when presented with issues that mirror the past. That is exactly what happened. Deciding to launch a new career in the military after a short term employment with the area school district, I was again given a golden opportunity to "use" freely. Most know that the military freely fosters the culture of alcohol. Although illicit substances are frowned upon, alcohol is the more viable option (at least in my situation). Let's just say I fit right in. The luggage that I had packed was literally bursting at the seams. My past demons were all back with friends. My bitterness with God that was initiated grew even more as time progressed. Eventually, my marriage was lost. I was actually forced by the situation to finish the academic career launched 13 years prior and had just ended five years before. That's right! Once again, I found myself back in the same area on the same campus where I found God to finally complete the coursework that I had started years back, NOT TO MENTION STILL FIGHTING THE DEMONS THAT I THOUGHT I LEFT THERE. I ended up back in the same place with old classmates who were either employed with the institution or working on various other certifications. I was only lacking 30 hours to finish. Lord knows I couldn't even pass by the financial aid office!!! Luckily, I had access to my G.I. Bill that would provide me the much-needed opportunity to finalize and create this milestone in my life. I had a few bumps in the road along the way, but I DID IT!!!!

I had finally finished college and was finally prepared, WITH BAGGAGE, but it worked. It was time to close one chapter and move to the next by moving back to my hometown. It was like I had never left. However, my addiction had begun to cause me health problems. It had finally caught up with me. We've heard it before. Eventually, it will all catch up with you. I was not taking care of myself at all, and to top it off, I had developed a "spice" habit. Yep. I had become addicted to "spice." For those of you who don't know, "spice" is a slang term for a new drug that had hit the streets that was at one time legally sold in stores. It was sold as synthetic marijuana, but it caused me to hallucinate oftentimes, which really scared me. Eventually, I had a terrible trip on it one night, and the drug made me hallucinate and think that the STOP SIGN on the street corner started talking to me and asked me, "WHATCHA GETTING READY DO BRUH?"

There was no way I was about to have a conversation with a traffic sign in hell. At that moment, I literally blinked, and I was in Madame Laveau's Voodoo Shop in the French Quarter in New Orleans. I blinked again, and I was passed out on the floor where I lived at the time. Crazy, huh? Fast-forwarding to the present, I've learned that living for God in the midst of making mistakes in life has profited me in many ways. I ended up receiving so much in return for making a change. Although I've experienced my share of challenges with sobriety, as I write this passage to the reader, I am celebrating a new wife of 7 years, a family of 4, and ONE ON THE WAY, all while sustaining a career of self-employment in entertainment and empowering others to stay on the straight and narrow even when it seems complicated.

I have to attribute my perseverance throughout all of this to become rooted in the Word Of God. Jeremiah 33:3 states, "Call unto me, and I will answer thee, and show thee great and mighty things, which thou knowest not." This scripture made me push hard when I wanted to quit! If you really desire to know your next move on your journey, I urge you to seek God. He has all the answers. Develop a strong relationship with him, EVEN WHEN YOU MAKE MISTAKES.

My mother's death, Sylvia Kay Dorsey, hurt me deeply, and it inspired me to change my life even more (AFTER I ALMOST DRANK MYSELF TO DEATH!!!LOL!!!). She instilled so many Godly principles within me before she left this world. She always said, "One day, you and your story will touch the masses."

Well, Mom! I guess you were right! Whether it's by a joke, a song, or a book, I think you hit the nail on the head. My father will probably read this and say, "Hell, I guess he forgot about me." No, Dad! I didn't. You've told me for years that "Life is the best teacher, but you can only live it once."

I guess this means I'm still being taught! Much love, John Lee Dorsey! Absorb, apply, and overcome! Peace.

About
C. Richaude Dorsey

C. Richaude Dorsey is an Actor, Stand-up Comedian, Jazz Artist, Fashion Stylist, and Motivational Speaker hailing from Gulfport, Mississippi. In 2012 he created and launched ``Ambience" (rebranded in 2020 as TEAM AMBIENCE, LLC), an organization representing music, fashion, comedy, & inspirational speaking. He is a proud alumnus of Alcorn State University, where he studied Psychology and Social Science. As a standup comedian, he has had the opportunity to share the stage and perform with various Celebrity Comedians, such as Joe Clair (former BET Comic View Host) and Shawty of BET

Comic View). In addition, he has hosted Celebrity Fashion Shows alongside Jocelyn Hernandez of VH-1's Love and Hip Hop. Although he has a passion for music that has spanned over thirty years, this has not overshadowed his passionate love for today's youth. This display of love has fueled his involvement in being a former member of Harrison County Drop Out Prevention Board. He was able to provide the administration with key points and methods of focus to prevent the youth of the area from becoming statistics. He served his country in the United States Army for a total of nine years. He is also a member of the Omega Psi Phi Fraternity, Inc. C. Richaude Dorsey was recently nominated for Comedian Of The Year for the Gulf Coast Gospel Music Awards (GCGMA) which is an internationally recognized organization that caters to the Gospel/Kingdom industry. C. Richaude also serves as Youth Pastor for his local assembly at House of Healing International Ministries under Apostle Joshua P. Smith. He testifies that God's grace and favor have allowed him to showcase his innate skills, talents, and abilities with the world through various platforms.

Connect with C. Richaude Dorsey

Book Him: bit.ly/richaudedorsey
E-mail: teamambience@gmail.com

The Devil You Know
By John Windsor

For the first time in my life, I am cuffed and in the backseat of a patrol car. Is this really about to happen? It's a chilly fall evening in Washington State, 1997. The policemen have just told me that they are going to have to take me downtown to the station because, well, someone has to leave. If someone has to leave, why didn't they just ask me to leave the house? Why the cuffs? Forget all of that; why are they making *ME* leave? I called *THEM!* Man, these cuffs are tight.

From the backseat, I ask the officers, "Am I going to the station to be questioned? Why can't I just go to a friend's house during a cool down period if you just need someone to leave?"

The female officer from the front seat replies, "Sir, I am going to need you to sit back and be quiet; you are being arrested."

"Wait, for what?" I shouted.

The female officer was in no mood to entertain questions, especially from me, an alleged wife beater. "Sir, sit back and shut up. If you refuse to comply, I will be forced to use this," she shouts back while pointing a can of pepper spray toward my face. Stunned and in complete disbelief, I sit back and comply.

A hundred things are racing through my head at a million miles per minute. Random thinks like: I cannot believe that I am about to become a statistic. My children just watched their dad handcuffed and taken away, how is that going to affect them? Holy shit! If I get my phone call, who am I going to call? I cannot call my parents; they are not speaking to me right now because I married *THIS* girl. Oh my God! What will my command do when they find out

I have been arrested? Are they going to kick me out of the military, and I didn't even do anything? Ahhhhhh!!!! How did I even get into this mess? I know how..., I should have never called the police! This is my fault! If I had dealt with this situation alone, I would not be on my way to the station right now. But..., on the contrary, how much worse would it have gotten? She had already broken every dish in the kitchen, and I am now sporting a fresh cut on my face from the chattered champagne bottle that she threw at my head. My leg is still throbbing from when she threw the iron at me, and I blocked it with my thigh. Since she couldn't land any kicks or punches, she decided to club me with my golf club until I was able to get to the kitchen to call the police. Would she have continued to press the attack until I really was forced to defend myself?

We have finally arrived at the police station, but I am not being taken in the front door; it appears that they are taking me straight to jail. Just as fast as I was escorted out of my house, I was being pushed into the jail. No explanation, no warning, no nothing. As soon as I am inside, I am asked to strip down to my underwear and socks immediately. I begin to protest, "Am I being thrown in jail? I didn't do anything!"

They ignore me, then punch an orange jumpsuit into my chest. Two officers hold me while I am fingerprinted and photographed. Then, they shove me, alone, into a holding cell. There are no tables, no chairs, just a cold concrete block to sit on. It's freezing and smells like fresh morning piss! Here, I would sit and wait for hours. I could see the processing area through a small window in the door, watching in horror as real criminals were being brought in. Some of these folks had some serious mental conditions, too, talking to themselves, yelling at people that were not there, and fighting with the police officers. I just simply could not believe that just this morning, I am an active duty Naval Engineer, upholding the highest military standards and traditions, and hours later, I am somehow an alleged wife beater. Yo, WTF!!!!

After about 3 hours of waiting, a correctional officer opens my door to the holding cell and finally escorts me out. He hands me a blanket and some slippers. I quickly ask, "Aye, man, what do I need these for?"

He states, "you are being escorted to the detention center. Follow me."

Before I know it, I am being led deeper and deeper into the jail until I am finally placed in a cell with roughly 30 people. None of whom appear to be here for the same reason I am. The corrections officer tells me to find a bunk, gives me a quick shove, and then slams the door behind me. Now, I stand like a confused child, confronted with the harsh reality of being locked away with real criminals. I find a top bunk next to a tiny window. Within minutes, I am approached by two guys, tatted from head to toe. "What they get you for, homie?" one of them asks.

Before I can speak, the other guy asks, "When's your court date?" I don't answer.

"Did they arrest you today? 'Cause Friday is the worse day to get arrested, homie, your court date won't be until next week, if you are lucky, hahaha?"

Blind rage begins to surge through my body as I am quickly overcome with the realization that I am in jail; who knows when or *if* I would ever get out. The rabbit hole just keeps getting deeper as now, fear begins to creep in, and my mind starts to play out scenarios. Is there a chance that this really goes to court? What if no one believes me? What if she decides that because I called the cops on her, she is going to continue to lie? This can't be innocent until proven guilty because, look at me, I am innocent and behind bars. What if I have to prove my innocence? Man, I can't afford a lawyer! Without even realizing it, I completely tune out everything in the cell, including the two guys in front of me, as I began to contemplate what had just happened. There had to be some signs or subtle hints that this could be a potential outcome. Because seriously everyone, and I mean everyone, told me that being with her was a terrible idea. But I tuned them out because I knew something that they didn't.

I began to peer out of that tiny cell window and reflect back. I thought back to how we met in high school and how she pursued me relentlessly. I thought about how I ignored her advances until one day, I got a call from her. She had been expelled from school and sent to attend school in DC. There she met a guy at her new school. She went on to explain how this flashy young man lured her in with his fancy car, befriended her, and later date raped her. In this scenario, she had become pregnant and was afraid to tell her parents; the one thing that she had decided, though, was that she was keeping the child. She explained how she was afraid to go to the police because she was afraid of him, and she did not know what he would do if she told her teachers, the police, or her parents. She said that she was terrified that she would end up missing. So, she swore me to secrecy. At that moment, I became determined that since she had the courage to tell me before she told anyone else, that I would be a real friend. Someone that won't disappear when things get tough. So, I became her confidant, and we spoke every day. For five solid months, she hid this secret from her parents. During this time, I did everything that I could do to be there for her until she could actually muster up the courage to tell her parents. It was through this "trauma bonding" several months later that we began a relationship. Yes, I was that guy. The one who would don the cape of the "White Knight" to save a damsel in distress. Honestly, I thought it to be the honorable thing to do. I felt as though God knew my heart and that he would see us through to greener pastures.

The first red flag had to be when her alleged rapist showed up at the hospital to see his child. Yep, you heard that right! He showed up at the hospital. After going to the nursery and taking a good look at his child in the nursery, he had seen enough. The father looked directly into my eyes and said, "Good luck with that," pointing to the room where my girlfriend lay sleeping. He politely shook my hand and walked off, never to be seen again. If I am being honest, at that moment, I wanted to do this man serious harm. After all, he is the man that raped my girl. The unmitigated gall of this guy! But, I was totally disarmed by the irony of that moment. And too, at that moment, it filled me with a sneaky suspicion that I was not fully grasping the gravity of this moment.

Sitting helplessly in this cell was the first time I had actually called into question his potential innocence. Never once up to this moment had I ever questioned the validity of the story that my wife fed me that day, and she allowed me to sacrifice everything to "save" her. I mean, I fought and distanced myself from my own family because I wanted to ensure that she was protected from the world. Protected from judgment. That she had an opportunity for the life that had been so ruthlessly stripped from her. But..., what if she lied? What if she skillfully manipulated me into believing that she had been raped so that I would do everything that I had? What if she looked at me and saw a neon sign on my forehead flashing "Sucker"? Wait, is this why she swore me to secrecy? Did he really rape her? I mean, let's get real, what rapist shows up to the hospital to examine the product of his crime? Who lies like that? Have I now become *him*? Not a rapist, but a wife beater! Oh, God! Please Lord, no! What if they put her in front of a jury? I won't stand a chance!

Over the next several, tumultuous hours I continue to reflect on the many red flags that had presented themselves over the years leading up to this melt-down. I thought about how, prior to joining the military, I had designs on one day becoming a doctor. I thought about how I worked throughout high school as a barber to pay my own college tuition, cash. Can you imagine the self-discipline that it would take a 16–17-year-old to save the majority of his pay to fund an education? Further, how I dropped out of school for a semester to step up for my girl in a way that no one had before, because now..., now she is having *my* baby. She constantly complained that she never had a chance for college because she was raped and had to raise a child. I thought about how I swiftly swooped in, paid for her classes, cash, and babysat her child while she attended. Personally, I thought that this is what a real man would do for his family. Sadly, the sacrifices that were made were only for her to flunk out and waste that opportunity.

As my daughter grew in her belly, I began to see with some clarity the large financial burden that was awaiting me. So, I decided that I would drop all the way out of school and work full time to fully financially support my child and this new family that I had started. I wanted to be accountable, and I wanted to be present. I sincerely wanted to be the man my mom worked so hard for me to eventually become. Responsible, accountable, and a leader. A man of integrity. I quickly learned, though, that during school and work hours, there is no one coming into the shop for a haircut, which means that I was not really making any more money working full-time as a barber. So, at the urging of my family, I made the smartest decision I could have made for my life, and that was to join the Navy. It was a guaranteed paycheck, right? My daughter would get excellent medical coverage, right? I would finally be financially stable enough to support a family and marry my girlfriend. I saw this as the perfect opportunity, a perfect fit for my situation! There is no way that this could fail..., right?

Red flag number two had to be how she showed up in Missouri with two children on her hip (her son and my daughter) and two trash bags of clothes to the base where I was attending "A" school following Bootcamp. She had no money, no transportation, no place to stay, and no plan. As a man, what do you do in this situation? Your baby and baby mom are at the gate and have apparently voluntarily become homeless. Do you leave them standing at the gate and send word for them to turn around and go home or do you step up and figure it out? Lord help, me! Who does this?!? Especially with no warning at all! Seriously, cell phones were not really a thing back then, but the Postal Service was. There were pay phones, tell-a-grams, girl, I don't care if you have to send a carrier pigeon. Under no circumstances should I ever have learned of your decisions because you are standing homeless at the gate. So, seemingly, I had no choice.

I did what I had to do. Although I was technically not allowed to leave the base due to my training requirements, I begged my superiors for an opportunity to handle this. They reluctantly granted me the opportunity to get this taken care of while simultaneously giving me a side-eye as though there were not entirely sure that I didn't plan this. Methodically, I set her up, paid for a hotel for my last six weeks of school, and gave her money for food, diapers, and transportation. The Navy, to this point, had not changed me. It had filled me with much more resolve, much more of a desire to be the best man that I could be. So, within a week, we were married and preparing to head to my first duty station as a family. A few weeks later, I was informed that there would be a new addition to our family. 20 years old and the father of three children!

Red Flag number three was more complex, her behavior during this new pregnancy. Her behavior really began to change and became far more erratic and controlling. Now, stationed in Seattle, Washington, my wife and I were in a whole new environment. We were getting a fresh start. Starting a family in the Greater Northwest, but something was not right. She was not happy. We had become a more traditional family where I worked, bringing home the biggest wage that I had ever made while she stayed home and tended to the children. I graduated top of my class in "A" school, which guaranteed a swift promotion from E-1 to E-4, locking in an even better salary. But the pressures of being a stay-at-home mom of two began to take its toll. She consistently stated her displeasure of how unfair that it was that she was stuck at home while I was able to go to work outside of the house. She felt like she was being subjugated into a lesser role just because she was a woman. So, trying to be understanding, we took a shot at her working in the evenings while I tended to the children. She took on three different jobs and was fired, or "quit" within 30-60 days at each one. She began to smoke and drink heavily while she was pregnant with our child. I confronted her and addressed this behavior. Do you think that it had any impact? Hell Naw! It actually made her behavior worse. How dare I address her behavior as though she was some child. "You ain't my daddy! I'm grown. You don't tell me what to do!" she would exclaim.

For months, this behavior continued until one day, enough was enough. By this time, we had finally welcomed our new child into the world. The expenses of taking on a third child had forced me to take on more work. Two additional jobs, to be more exact. After all, I am the man of the house, and making ends meet was supposed to be my job. Quite frankly, if I had considered any other alternative, it was now abundantly clear that I could not count on her to work or keep a job. This brings me to the events before me.

This particular day, returning home from a 14-hour shift, I opened the door to screaming children. It was apparent that my children had not been fed, nor had they been attended to all day. My children were wearing such filthy diapers that it was clear that they had not been touched all day long. I had no choice but to attend to them, changing them and get them under control immediately. After I was able to settle them down, my wife emerged from the bedroom. She walks past me and proclaims that she is going out. I looked at her up and down and yelled, "Really?"

She yelled back, "That's right, really! You haven't been stuck here with them all day with no car! It's your turn. I keep telling you, you AINT MY Daddy, and don't make me say it again!" She defiantly brushes past me on her way to get her coat.

In a rage, I yell back, "Well, it ain't like your fat ass does anything around here anyway. So, be gone then!" Admittedly, I should not have said that. But I had said it, and I could not take it back.

This brief fit of anger seemed to cause some sort of a visible break somewhere deep inside her. She instantly started picking up anything she could find and hurling it at my head. When she ran out of things to throw, she rushed me and attempted to punch and kick me. She found my golf clubs in the corner and started clubbing me with my driver until I snatched it away from her. She then went into the kitchen and started breaking every dish she could get her hands on. I pled with her to calm down, but she wouldn't. She was screaming and crying uncontrollably. I didn't know what to do, so I called the police. I explained that she was hysterical and I needed someone to come help me calm her down. She could hear that I was calling the police, and the hysterics in the kitchen immediately stopped. She marched to the bedroom and picked up the call from there. Once again hysterical, she begins to tell the 911 operator that I was crazy and that I was beating on her, that she was bleeding and that she needed help. The truth was that she had gotten a C-section weeks ago and had previously broken open the stitches. This was her second time. No doubt, attempting to fight me and hit me with my golf clubs. Within minutes, the police showed up at the house, banging on the door. I opened the door to policemen, guns drawn, in position to kick the door in. The cops separated us in different parts of the house, questioned us, and decided to take me in after about 30 minutes of questioning.

Lucky for me, I was arrested on a Thursday night and thankfully arraigned late Friday afternoon. I arrive at the hearing terrified, knowing that this could get a lot worse really fast. When my case reaches the judge he asks me, "how did you plead to the charges?"

I am terrified because I have no lawyer and we all know how black men have fared in the judicial system. "Not guilty, your honor," I replied. Fortunately, the prosecutor interrupted explaining to the judge that the State didn't think that they had enough evidence and had no choice but to dismiss as the spouse had not pressed charges at that time. The judge allowed it and released me to the custody of my Commanding Officer, who was present. Oh my God, I was free! The entire 24-hour ordeal taught me that you never truly understand how quickly your freedom can be stripped from you, innocent or guilty, until you experience something like this.

My Commanding Officer had a couple of Chief Petty Officers take me to my house to get my things. One of them called my wife and told her I was coming to get my things. When I arrived, one Chief escorted me to my bedroom to pack my belongings while the other kept my wife separated from me so that there would be no further incidents. From the other room, all I could hear were the cries of my children and the wailing of my wife begging me not to leave. It was truly heart-wrenching. I had never heard my daughter cry this way before, not like this, and it broke me down. The seething anger inside of me was transformed to pure agony. I simply could not ignore the pain that this was causing my children. In a flash, I could see their futures without me and I could also see my future without them. So, I caved and decided to stay. For them. Statistically, it is said that a domestically abused spouse will return to their abuser on average seven times before they finally attempt to leave for good. For me, this was one of the first times. Little did I know how much this critical decision would cost me and my children.

For the next eight years, I continued to work on that marriage, pouring all of myself into the relationship, attempting to create the best representation of life for my children. But the physical and emotional abuse continued and got exponentially worse over the years, creating many new chapters of suffering. I felt totally disarmed in my ability to fight back based on the perspective that any attempt to do so could cost me everything and rob my children of their futures. After ten years of marriage, I broke down and prayed that God would show me the way. Ultimately, he showed her the door. The divorce robbed my children of a full-time father, their education, and landed them in a less than desirable community. I was barely able to hold on to my sanity after I lost my children. I was in financial ruin. I lost my family, my children, my house, and quite nearly my career practically overnight.

A few years later, after consistent prayer, I was eventually introduced to the woman of my dreams. She found me like Moses, wandering through the desert, starving, tired and broken. Like me, she was also a product of an abusive relationship. She, like Zipporah did for Moses, introduced to my life a world of peace, as well as two beautiful daughters. Together though, through God's love, we were strengthened and made whole. That love resonated and re-aligned our family. My wife and I put a premium on education and worked hard to provide the best model for our children. Ten years later, my dreams for my family have been realized. Today, as a family, we are the proud owners of 13 degrees, two thriving businesses, four grandchildren, and a bright future of possibilities. Although my children from my previous marriage are all grown up, they still bear the scars of their past life. Thankfully, they are learning not to let their past alter their futures. I am so proud of them!

About
John Windsor

A native of Gulfport, MS, John Windsor, Jr. has deep roots in the Washington DC metropolitan area, commonly known as the DMV (DC/Maryland/Va). Mr. Windsor is a two-time graduate of the University of Charleston, earning a Bachelor's of Science Degree in Organizational Leadership and Management as well as a Master's of Business Administration (MBA). An active-duty Navy Senior Chief with 26 years of service to his credit, he has received several commendations for his humanitarian efforts during several natural disasters including Hurricane Katrina, the 2010 Haitian earthquake, the

2011 Fukushima tsunami and most recently the COVID-19 pandemic.

John Windsor, Jr. is a multi-faceted leader who has had a very diverse military career, holding a myriad of titles ranging from Assistant Budget Analyst to Facilities Director to Congressional Liaison. Mr. Windsor is also a devoted husband to a successful entrepreneur and the father of 5 beautiful children.

Connect with John Windsor
Email: Ea3wind@yahoo.com
Facebook: www.facebook.com/john.windsor.921

When Your Silence Is Too Loud, Choose A Different Song By Alfred Wells Jr.

Events and actions help influence how we view and approach life situations. My father's suicide when I was eleven did not influence me as much as I thought. He woke me up in the middle of the night to give me an action to live out prior to his suicide that shaped my outlook on life. It has been thirty-six years since he came to me; his words on my bedside have never left my head, forever haunted by his request. My mom and dad married and divorced young; however, I was born between those three years. My mom soon discovered she was not the only woman pregnant by her husband. My brother was born a few months after me. My father would go on to have two more children with his girlfriend before allegedly killing her and committing suicide by a single gunshot wound to his head.

I was raised by a single parent; my mother, who exemplified love and sacrifice daily. She worked in a candy factory one city over, in southeast Louisiana in the 80s. During the early 1980's where I grew up, racism was widespread and very visible. My mother was continuously the target of ridicule, disparaging words, and unfair treatment. She was referred to as a "Nigger gal" often by her supervisor and co-workers. With only a high school diploma and without a specific trade, my nineteen-year-old mother needed to find a job quickly after she and my father separated. With a small mouth to feed and no regularly scheduled child support or assistance, we desperately needed to keep a source of steady income. She found a full-time job at the candy factory. In a small town, without any other options, she had no choice but to stay there and endure harsh and unfair treatment. She sacrificed her dignity to ensure I had the necessities...shelter, water, food, and clothing. The best part was that it didn't matter what happened at work; when she got home, she always had a smile for me; she loved me more than she loved herself.

My home was filled with love and an example of what hard work looks like. As I grew up, I maintained good grades and had a solid head on my shoulders. My grandfather provided an example of what a man looks like and how he provides for his family. Though my grandfather lived next door, and I saw him daily, he was not around me all the time; so, I saw other examples of how to provide for a family as well. I saw boys my age, no more than fourteen and fifteen, making more money than my mom and grandfather combined! I could not believe it and was more than intrigued. After a while, those same boys allowed me to hang out with them and watch them work. I will admit they worked hard—street entrepreneurs at their finest. Early mornings and late nights for some, while others had set hours. They taught me different things than my elders, such as be quiet and watch, and be leery of those you don't know, and more cautious of those you do. They taught me how to survive in the streets. I saw so many things, but my thoughts on love, trust, and women were cemented as I repeatedly saw guys set up to get robbed by their friends and especially by their girlfriends. I watched police plant drugs during a traffic stop or while frisking my friends. I cemented feelings of distrust when I saw friends shot or shot at by people we went to school with. I saw what hard work and love looked like in and out of my home. Despite the warm unwavering love in my home, the love outside distorted my definition and idea of what love was. I was leery of most and trusted no one. I left Louisiana before I got into serious trouble.

A year after joining the military, I was blessed with my daughter. Even though her mother and I didn't work out, I was active in her life even while living countries apart. A few years later, in love and married, I found out I was the father to another daughter from a previous relationship. Fast forward almost two decades later; I was excitedly awaiting the birth of my son. I vowed not to be an absent father like my father was to me. I have no doubt my dad loved me; however, like many, he had his vices which blinded his vision of love. I found his love distorted, but it was probably clear to him. After seven years, my wife and I divorced, but we moved to the same location. We both grew up without a father and understood the importance of having two parents in our life. She and I wanted more for our child than what was given to us...two-parent involvement and all it was going to take was communication, compromise, and sacrifice, which we both were committed to providing even after our marriage failed.

ALFRED WELLS JR.

After moving from Hawaii to Washington D.C., I worked a minimum of twelve-hour days/five days a week while enrolled in a full-time Master's Degree program and figuring out what single–parenting/co-parenting looked and felt like. It was tough, and I struggled daily. Trying to operate at the same intensity and passion as I did as a married man, but now as a single parent in a more demanding job, all with the shadow of my father looming over me and an unquenchable desire to be better than he was. I couldn't fail, so I endured. I hid my struggles and feelings while trying to establish myself in this new environment, determined to continue maintaining organizational excellence within my workspace. If I had nothing, I had work ethic and a chip on my shoulder that motivated me. To some people working while going to school and raising a child is easily managed, but it was overwhelming for me. Unfortunately, I was unaware of the damage I was inflicting on myself. Oftentimes, I would drop my son off at the child development center at 6:00 am and work until 5:30 pm before literally running out the door to pick up my three-year-old son before the center closed at 6 pm. My son was, at many times, the first kid at daycare and the last kid picked up. I hated it, but I didn't have any other way. I would pick him up and often return to work with an IPAD and snacks for him so I could finish up the day's tasks. I was literally burning both ends of the candle trying to survive at work and be a good dad.

Why work this hard? I worked for a wonderful boss who had a tenacious work ethic. She never asked me to match her schedule; however, first impressions are lasting impressions. I wanted to establish a connection early with her and my new team. My boss and I would attend the 5:30 am shift change and pass off important information to the team, and some days we were still there for the 8:30 pm shift change to do the same thing. Our days were long but rewarding, and I enjoyed doing my part to advance the team. After those long workdays, I would arrive home and immediately begin my school work. Being a full-time college student coupled with long exhausting military workdays was taxing mentally and physically. It was not uncommon to work on school assignments until 1:00 am, or 2:00 am, only to get up at 4:30 am. This went on for more than a year...then one day it stopped, suddenly.

One day, two coworkers that I had grown very fond of walked into my office for what I thought was one of their daily conversations. Honestly, I looked forward to their conversations each day. The conversations were a breath of fresh air. These two and I spoke often and had a great relationship; they had access to my calendar and helped schedule and modify my day based on my calendar and mission needs. They kept me on track in a time where my mind and time were often in disarray. I appreciated them and their work immensely. These two were instrumental to me staying on track and helping me meet deadlines. The atmosphere seemed different and not as lighthearted when they walked in that day. One asked, "how are you doing today?" I immediately answered, "I'm doing fine." I will admit I was a little uncomfortable for some reason. The two people who often eased my stressful day were serious but caring. The other coworker responded, "Are you sure?" I started laughing and said, "Of course, I'm sure."

By the age of fifty-five, my grandmother had both of her legs amputated, a false eye, and legally blind in the other, yet she smiled until the very end. She taught me so much about life, gratitude, and understanding someone always has it worse than you. Growing up with that mentality, I have always been appreciative of the smallest things, and I very rarely had a "pity party." The first time was when my dad died, and the second was when I experienced a significant emotional event a decade into my military career. Over the course of my 29-year military career, I developed a philosophy that "leaders don't have bad days; they have doors." Leaders cannot afford to dump their bad days onto those that rely on them to help, aid, or assist others.

Leaders self soothe behind their closed office doors and emerge ready to assist after they gather their composer. So, maybe now you can understand my laughter when they asked about my day because I was sure I was having a good day. I remember vividly like it was yesterday. I had assisted two people with a financial concern earlier that day and helped recoup more than three thousand dollars. I remember feeling accomplished and glad I was there to help. I also remember that I spoke with another individual in reference to his error in judgment and the repercussions from his decisions while assuring him that I would walk with him throughout the process. I remember being grateful to do my job and help those in need. Lastly, I assisted a member going through a divorce by advising her and directing her to a helping agency. Yes! I was having a typical good day, but that was not the question my coworkers wanted me to answer. They wanted to know "If I was doing alright," not how my day was going, how I was personally...not professionally. They caught me off guard and told me I had an appointment with our organization's doctor.

I laughed, just as boisterously as I laughed earlier. I looked at both of them, and to my surprise, their faces remained stoic. I knew they were serious. I felt a lump in my throat, and anger rose. Sadness, pain, and doubt filled my mind in a split second. I felt sweat run down my back. It seemed like minutes had passed but actually only seconds. I paused for a moment contemplating whether to kick them out of my office or not. I chuckled, called their bluff and called the doctor. To my surprise, the doctor verified he was standing by and would be expecting me in thirty minutes. I hung up the phone, stood up, and said "I'm not sure what you two are up to, but I'm heading over to see the doctor." I was calm on the outside, a ball of confusion and dismay on the inside. My insides screamed, my heart cried, but I held my head high like a good leader who doesn't have a bad day, at least that is what I told myself.

ALFRED WELLS JR.

I drove to the doctor's office and parked. Before getting out of my car, I pulled out my work phone and finalized a few actions that involved addressing a drinking and driving arrest, rescheduling an office visit, and sending a congratulatory message to a coworker and his spouse on the birth of their new baby. Work was my peace. I knew what work entailed, and it came easy to me. If I had nothing, I had work ethic, even if it was to my own demise. I buried myself in work. As you can see, I dealt with a wide range of emotions on a daily basis. I carried everyone's emotions with me. I turned my emotions off and carried theirs. It's what I did, and it's how I survived. Ironically, I won the most awards and had the most success when I was in my darkest moments.

After taking care of some last-minute business, I walk into the doctor's office. All of my coworkers and I share the same doctor, which was great for me and my line of business. My military job is equivalent to what the corporate world refers to as a Human Relations Manager. In the military, we are called First Sergeants, and we wear a diamond in the middle of our stripes. I always wanted to be a First Sergeant, also known as a "diamond." Much like the stones, diamonds are special and rare, small in number but strong in our capability to serve those in need.

At the time, I was the First Sergeant responsible for an elite team of policemen or security forces members who helped protect and secure the aircraft carrying the President of the United States, Vice President, Secretary of State, Secretary of Defense and

75

Chairman Joint Chiefs of Staff. Supporting and taking care of two hundred and eighty-three coworkers, who were responsible for escorting and securing the "Department of Defense Top 5", was a job I thoroughly enjoyed. I saw the importance of their mission, my role and received immediate gratification knowing I was an integral part of the team. There was no feeling like it. I was a part of something so much bigger than myself, serving those who protected our nation's leaders. A small town boy now trusted to care for Airmen!

The doctor's assistant took my vitals two times and noticed my high blood pressure. She made a note of it and told me the doctor would see me now. Normally, I stop by the doctor's office to discuss one of my teammates, so I skip the vitals portion, but this time I was seen as a patient and not as a guest, which is very different for me. I hated it. My vitals alarmed me, I didn't pay much attention to them before, but I remember the medical technician's look after the first reading. She was shocked and asked if my pressure was usually high.

The doctor asked how Wells, my last name, was doing...I immediately began to run down some of my questions concerning my teammates. How a coworker was doing was easy for me to answer. I thanked him for assisting someone with an appointment and providing a member a referral to see a medical specialist, and finally, I asked how I could assist my team better? After entertaining my questions and comments, he asked how Al, my first name, was doing. The room seemed to get smaller - he seemed to be much closer to me now. It was like he was in my personal space, but neither he nor I had moved. My chest tightened. My mind raced. I was trying to figure out what was going on because I immediately felt a rush of emotions as my eyes filled with water. I didn't know what was happening; I began to cry. Since my father died, I had not cried in front of anyone and definitely not another man. I was unable to control my tears and wondered what had just happened. I was filled with emotions I didn't know I had; I felt like someone had just tapped into my core and all of my bottled-up feelings began to flow like a geyser. The floodgates of emotions were opened. Emotions I had turned off so long ago that I forgot they were there. I forgot that I could feel.

That was the first time someone asked how I was doing personally and purposefully. Someone really wanted to know how I was doing, and it wasn't a checkbox question. His question wasn't a formality. It was genuine. During my daily activities, I exchanged greetings and salutations such as "Hello, how are you," and "Hi, what's going on?" with others but usually in passing. Usually, I am the person asking and waiting for answers so I can do my job.

The doctor's question was deliberate and purposeful. I felt like no one had asked me the way he did. The patient demeanor, soft spoken words, genuine concern, and attentive ear were all indicators that this person cared about what was going on in my life. He saw past my hard exterior. He was past my professional smile and concern for others. He saw past the stripes and diamonds. He saw a man who was broken and held together solely by the auspicious cover of work ethic. After a few minutes of uncontrollable tears, snot bubbles, and a complete ugly cry, I stopped. It was like I had been holding my breath trying to survive, and now I could exhale. We discussed the demands of work, single parenting/co-parenting, fatherhood, being a student and a leader was having on me...yep, and I began to cry again, and I let my tears flow. I don't think I could have stopped those tears even if I wanted to. My emotions had built up over time like the pressure in a volcano. Sadly, I was juggling so many things that I didn't realize I was on the verge of exploding. I had never experienced the tears and emotions I was feeling. It seemed as if I was not in control of my own thoughts and emotions.

The most important things were first, not letting my son down, and second, not letting my teammates down. I didn't consider not letting myself down, so it was easy to disregard personal signs of despair. I thought my despair was weakness. Growing up fatherless with a mother who left for work every day before I woke up and only saw me on school days right before the streetlights came on allowed me time to see what others did. I had a lot of time to myself. Where I grew up, older kids taught me a few things: Do not show emotions, keep your circle of friends tight, and most importantly, don't trust those that didn't grow up shooting marbles with you. In other words, if we don't have a long relationship, then I don't trust you. People had to earn my trust, but until then, everything someone did or said was analyzed, heavily analyzed. They were "suspect." A lesson that I was shown, not told, was men deal with things internally. I got that lesson early in life. "Lock it up" and "man up," ...so that was my mentality. I opened up to the young doctor against what I was taught. It was challenging to do. I would suffice to say it was one of the most challenging things I had to do in my life, but my silence was too loud, so I chose another song to survive. I had to; I needed to.

Internally, I was dealing with things I didn't think I had a problem with. It wasn't until that very moment that it hit me all at once, the death of my father. His suicide affected my mind and how I carried and conducted myself. I thought of some of my decisions as a teen, young adult, and actions well into my adulthood. My mind swarmed. I could see and feel how not dealing with and processing my father's suicide had silently affected my entire life—thoughts of relationships, personal and professional decisions: my contemplation of suicide after a traumatic situation. The longer I sat there, I realized some things bothered me that I previously didn't even know were an issue. I had disregarded the situation. I discovered and internalized some of the reasons I had not gotten a good night's rest in decades. It was like watching a replay of my life and seeing how suppressing my feelings affected so much of my life. I knew then I lived in silence for too long, and there was no choice but to change my song. The doctor gave me great advice, discussed coping techniques, prescribed medications, and referred me to someone I could speak with to better my mental health. I felt like I was going to breathe again. I was no longer suffocating in my own silence.

My father placed a heavy burden on me the night he committed suicide; I remember him kneeling next to my bed as he woke me.

He told me, "I am going away for a long time, and I may not be back."

I asked him how long he would be gone, and he told me he was probably not coming back. He told me, "take care of your brothers and sister. They love you, so be sure to take care of them and keep them close."

He hugged me, and that was the last time I saw him alive. Imagine an eleven year old child getting this direction from their parent; as the older sibling, I felt empowered yet lost. As a child, I could only do so much. Shortly after my dad died, my brothers and sister moved away, so I could not take care of them as my father asked while basically on his deathbed. Even after thirty-six years, I have only spoken to my brother and sister three or four times, and I have never talked to my youngest brother. Not speaking to them or having a relationship with them bothers me to this day. At the time, I felt I had not lived up to my father's wishes nor his expectations to look after them. I carried that weight for years. My father had only asked one thing of me, and I was not able to do it. Now that I am older and wiser, I realize it isn't my burden to bear. Over the years, as family and friends have needed me, it weighed on my heart if I couldn't help them. I also felt that I wasn't enough; I wasn't worth my dad staying around to watch me grow up. I adopted, harbored, and became intimate with an, "I am not enough mentality," which plagued me well into recent years.

The lesson I learned not to trust people was ingrained in me, etched into my being. DO NOT TRUST...It played on repeat in my mind. Don't trust people, especially those close to you. Especially to those close to you. They always leave. They. Always. Leave. I loved and later resented my father for placing such a heavy burden on me. He was close to me and hurt me the most, the task was too much for me, so I internalized my feelings and never displayed nor discussed my hurt and pain...I just dealt with it on my own, silently.

The lessons I learned damaged my personal relationships; I never fully gave myself to anyone because I didn't fully trust them. I did not communicate well...hell, I did not communicate at all. I could discuss surface situations, but when it came to matters of the heart, I was dead silent. As a child and while in a long-term relationship, I was told I would end up just like my father. I trusted this person but again, as my life kept teaching me, only those closest to you can hurt you the most. She hit me in my soul with those words mainly because I never expected her to say them. Physical bruises go away, but emotional scars and wounds linger and don't heal as quickly if they heal at all. During this relationship, I was not the most faithful man, and this person knew of my father's womanizing. She levied the same thoughts and criticisms on me, which, sadly, may not have been too far fetched. I knew one thing; I did not want to end up like my father. He shot himself after shooting and killing his girlfriend for over ten years. I would not let that be me.

The years of bottled-up thoughts and emotions led me to a diagnosis of anxiety and depression. I wasn't raised with men that had diagnosed mental conditions. I was walking around helping and assisting others and didn't know I was the one in dire need of help. Because I didn't talk and was accustomed to ignoring my thoughts for years, my inner self was screaming for help, and my two emotionally attuned coworkers heard my screams. Silent screams, screams at a pitch so distinct, that only someone who is emotionally in tune and selflessly concerned could hear. I chose to speak with someone, prioritized my life, and sought help instead of remaining silent. Internalizing my thoughts and emotions was damaging to me and those around me; *when my silence was too loud, I chose another song*. Now I am healing and finding happiness in ways I didn't know I could.

About
Alfred Wells, Jr

L eadership is the harmonious sum of the qualities of intellect, human and emotional intelligence, and moral character enabling a person to positively inspire a group of people. Compassionate and unyieldingly devoted to exuding the sum of leadership traits is the leader, Alfred Wells Jr.

Alfred Wells Jr is an author, advocate, business guru, and an Air Force Chief Master Sergeant, with an irrefutable commitment to helping others see their worth and potential. He is currently servicing military personnel and civilian members as the Senior Enlisted Leader of the 89th Communication Squadron. He is the principal advisor to the commander, on policies affecting 194 personnel. He advises on matters regarding quality of life, morale, health, welfare and mission execution of the organization's workforce. He has served as Human Relations manager for a total of 1300+ personnel. While hosting an impressive career, it is his commitment in developing and coaching others to realize their truest potential that motivates his service.

Alfred's Mantra is simple: God gave us two ears and one mouth so we can do twice the listening. To effectively help others, we must listen.

Alfred Wells Jr. 's tenacious work ethic is supported with a regard for higher learning as he has obtained honors as a Summa Cum Laude graduate with a bachelor's degree in Information Technology Management, Associates Degrees in, Avionics Systems Technology, Human Resource Management and Information Systems. He also has top tier certification in Security +.

Today, Alfred Wells Jr. is one of the top 1% of leaders, accomplishing more than 29 years of experience-based leadership, coaching and team building in the world's largest military. An accomplishment that while praised greatly by some was achieved by overcoming adversity through hard work and an undying will to be better. Alfred inspires many, advising them that even after you fail you can overcome and ultimately succeed; to be a guiding light for others suffering through tough times. He desires to inspire others by sharing relatable experiences; reminding them of their greatness and that they can survive and be successful. He is also the Founder and CEO of A Lion's Tale, LLC. The mission of A Lion's Tale® is to remind others we all have a story and we all have overcome some type of adversity, some more than others.

It is a story of how we "Failed.Overcame.Succeeded.®" We have failed or been knocked down, but we rise, adjust our crowns and stand as KINGS and QUEENS!

When Alfred is not out advocating for those navigating a storm or tough time, he is an active figure to his communal body, a son, beloved father of three, and dedicated partner and friend.

Alfred Wells Jr. Leader. Advocate. Entrepreneur.

Connect with Alfred Wells Jr.

FB: https://www.facebook.com/alfred.wells.35
Email: alionstalellc@gmail.com

My Breakthrough
By Fabian Cardona

had this spot on the island I really loved visiting during lunchtime. It was a cliff on the southeast side of the island. This was the kind of place where young couples used to go and park their cars most weekends in the afternoons to see the sunset, where tourists would flock to looking for the perfect shot of the ocean and the town's marina, or where people like me would go to find peace, solace, and a place to think or clear my mind at lunchtime. The cliff overlooked the old town with its picturesque homes and cobblestone roads. From there, you could see the bay full of yachts and fishing boats, kids playing in the park, and on a clear day, you could see for miles and miles and appreciate the grandness of the Atlantic Ocean. The cliff must have been at least 400 feet high, and the sound of the ocean's waves crashing on the rocks down below provided me with a sort of peace and tranquility desperately needed, especially on days when work was crazy and stressful.

I remember this cold, windy day in December like it was yesterday. I grabbed my lunch box and rushed to my car, heading to the cliff. This day, in particular, was very different than others. I dealt with backlash from a long-drawn-out readiness inspection; everyone wanted to stop by my office and complain about the smallest things. One of my young Airmen was in trouble with the local police, and on top of work-related issues, which seemed to be the norm at this location, I was also having marital problems with my wife at the time; I had recently discovered the reason why she had been acting totally different since we arrived at our new home duty station; I found out the disturbing truth and our relationship had taken on a very rocky outlook, to say the least. On top of all that, on this specific day, I was also notified that I would have to go to Iraq in a few months. This would be my second deployment to that barren land I had come to detest due to many reasons; I had already been there seven years ago during the war. This deployment would be my fourth total and my third in less than four years, and I, for one, did not want to miss another birthday; I didn't want to miss another father-daughter dance, nor another little league or basketball game. It is true that when it rains, it pours; it truly felt as if I was living through the perfect storm. During the drive to the cliff, I kept telling myself, "why me there are so many other people they could send? What about my kids, and with all that is happening right now in my personal life, this deployment could not have gotten here in the worst time!"

When I got into my car, I felt like I was carrying an elephant on my shoulders; they were heavy and sored, my head felt like it was going to explode, and I felt sick to my stomach. I was furious!! I kept telling myself this was not fair, mainly because the current location where I was stationed was not supposed to support deployments due to the nature of its mission.

Still, somehow the military had found a loophole, and I was once again tagged to go "down range." My mind just kept bouncing from one issue to the next. All the problems were just piling up, one on top of the other without end. A few minutes into my drive, this song came over the radio, and as the music played, I unconsciously started to hyperventilate; I didn't know what was happening, and out of nowhere, I felt the urge just to scream! I faded away, and it felt like my mind took me into another dimension, another time and place; my mind took me to a time when I was in Iraq the first time, suddenly murky memories from seven years ago started taking over me, I was completely lost in the past.

It was March 2003, and I drove a Humvee through the desert. It was over 120 degrees; we were wearing full chemical protective gear plus body armor; our destination was Baghdad. We crossed the border into Iraq over 18 hours before, but it felt more like we had been driving for two weeks straight. We only stopped to refuel at certain classified spots along the way as we trailed behind some armored vehicles called Bradley fighting vehicles, or tank killers as some soldiers called them, and a few Abraham tanks. Captain "Z" was my only passenger; he was an Air Force lawyer I met in Kuwait before crossing the border. When I first met Captain. Z I thought he was dull and boring, and I was already dreading the trip, but boy was I completely mistaken. He ended up having a wealth of knowledge, he was a history buff (and I loved history), and although he spoke softly, he was a very funny and entertaining man; he definitively helped me stay awake with the stories, jokes, and jeopardy games the entire time I had been at the wheel.

Suddenly I heard Captain Z shout, "Cardona, wake up!!" He was trying to wake me up as I dozed off and started drifting off the road.

I came back from my micro nap, and I said, "Sorry, Captain, I am awake. I'm fine, I promise."
Then he said, "I know what else we can do to help you stay awake, I am going to sing a song, and you are going to guess who sings the song."

He started vocalizing songs, and I guessed the song titles and the artists. After a while, he started humming a catchy tune, to which I joined in in singing and humming. We were having a blast when suddenly, a warning call came over the radio saying we needed to stop immediately and take cover as we had hit a pocket of enemy resistance.

We immediately jumped out of the Humvee, grabbed our ammunition, and tried to prepare for the worst as we took cover behind the wheels of the truck; form there, we could hear the unfolding battle as the fire, fight, and the explosions shook the ground just up the road from where we were. While we checked our equipment, we started going through possible scenarios and remembering our training on devising escape routes, cover, concealment, and rendezvous points.

We must have been there maybe 30-45 minutes, but it felt like an eternity. Finally, the "all clear" came through the radio, and we thanked God as we said to each other we could not believe we had not taken any direct fire. We got back in the truck and started to move slowly, and passed right through the area of the battle. We could see the total devastation that had ensued in that stretch of road; we could not believe our eyes! Along the road, we saw a handful of white Iraqi Toyota trucks and other enemy equipment; all was blown to pieces, some still on fire; it was total pandemonium, then a horrible smell took over.

"What is that smell?" I asked out loud. As I continued to drive, trying to maneuver through the debris of blown vehicles and equipment, I panned side to side and was able to discover the cause of the smell. It was enemy soldiers that laid there in between the remains of their vehicles. Some were completely charred, some still in flames, and some only pieces remained; it was total carnage. On a few of the bodies, I could see the horror frozen on their faces as they lived their last seconds on this earth when the tank killers delivered the unavoidable punishment. This was hell on earth, I wish I had looked away, but I couldn't. Oddly enough, I was drawn to these horrific images maybe because never in my life had I witnessed the destruction of this magnitude; I was an eyewitness to the atrocities of war for the first time. I looked over at Capt. Z, we both had tears in our eyes...a few minutes went by in total eerie silence, then we started humming the song again.

We finally arrived at our destination after a few grueling days of convoying. Between the fire fights and explosions, dodging scud missiles, wearing chemical suits in 120-degree heat, and sandstorms, we were ready to set up camp and rest. Our first home was Baghdad International Airport or Saddam International as it was known back then. We set up a temporary camp in the airport, which was adjacent to Saddam's Palace compound, as we waited for EOD personnel to clear the palace compound of unexploited ordinance so we could set up a more permanent base. The tank killers and tanks continued as they took on different missions, with the exception of two Bradleys which were left behind to provide force protection for our camp. In charge of guarding the gate were two young Army privates, Jim and Todd; they were no older than maybe 19 or 20 years old. That day, they came to me and boasted about how their sergeant had trusted them to perform such an important detail; this was a big deal for them.

I met Jim and Todd when we were still in Kuwait before the war started. Since our schedules were almost the same, we used to meet regularly at the chow hall (dining facility) there; we talked just about anything, about how the Air Force always had the best chaw halls, equipment and how they, being in the Army, always wished had joined the Air Force instead. We talked a lot about sports, especially about baseball and the old rivalry between the Yankees and the Red Socks; we were constantly reminiscing about home; I had really liked those kids as they reminded me of when I had first joined the military, so I decided to take them under my wing.

The next morning I was filling out inspection forms in the maintenance tent, which was located about fifty yards from the gate; I was drinking my coffee humming *that* song when a loud explosion startled me. The emergency siren started blasting, and the first thing that popped into my mind was that enemy forces were attacking us. I immediately donned my gas mask and helmet, grabbed my rifle, and started low crawling outside the tent. Once outside the tent, another soldier tapped me on my helmet and yelled, "we need some help over here, come on!"

I got up and started running after him as we headed towards the gate. Once we got to the gate, a few soldiers were kneeling on the ground performing first aid next to two injured soldiers.

The Army Sergeant in charge requested a SITREP (situational report), and one of the soldiers said that we had had an accidental discharge from one of the Bradleys. I was still trying to catch my breath since I was still wearing my gas mask. I removed the gas mask and approached the gate only to see that one of the injured soldiers was missing most of his head; his brains were spattered on the sand, blood everywhere! Next to him laid another soldier with a gaping wound to his neck. His arms stretched out, reaching for other people crying for help.

As he called for help, I could hear air escaping from his neck wound while blood would just spray out in an uncontrolled way. Suddenly realized that the poor soldier crying for help on the ground was Jim, and next to him lay the lifeless body of Todd. We tried to stop Jim from bleeding out, but there was nothing else we could do. Jim passed away, still trying to call for help, slowly fading away as we carried him to the helicopter. It was there that I knew my life would never be the same.

I had no idea I had arrived at the cliff, nor how long I had been sitting in my car, all I could think of were those charred bodies left in pieces, their dead faces, Todd's lifeless body, and Jim crying for help as he died. I could feel my heart pounding in my chest, I was crying profusely, and then my mind switched back to all the problems I was having that day. I felt totally detached, as if there was no world out there for me. I opened the door and walked towards the front of the car, parked close to the cliff's edge.

As I stood there in front of my car on that day, I gazed at the waves crashing on the rocks down at the bottom. It was windy and very cold, but yet I was sweating profusely under my jacket, my heart continued to pound in my chest, and I kept trying to catch my breath. Unexpectedly these dark thoughts started to take over my mind, thoughts I had never had before. I told myself, "this needs to end." I found myself asking if this could be the answer to all that was happening to me.

"Let me finish this now," I felt totally overwhelmed.

I kept repeating to myself there was nothing else I could do. I did not have answers, I could not find solutions to any of these problems, nor did I know the meaning behind all this feeling of sorrow, desolation, emptiness, and loneliness; I felt I didn't have a way out; I didn't know what else to do.

"Daddy, daddy! Look at the birdies!" I heard this little girl say in a pure and enthusiastic way as she ran toward the grassy area where a few picnic tables were located on the cliff.

It must have been her sheer happiness and the excitement in her voice that snapped me back into reality from the darkness. I sat on the hood of my car and watched as they took pictures of the seagulls and other birds as they fed on the bread the little girl was throwing at them. As the little girl continued to laugh and talk, my two kids came to mind, my babies; they were so little back then. Quickly the dark thoughts began to be replaced by memories of my little ones, our tickle fights and how they used to fight to see who could take my boots off the fastest after I got home from work, and how my son waited there to show me how much better he had gotten at our favorite video game. My eyes got teary again, and my anger and rage turned into shame; I was ashamed that I was quitting, I was embarrassed that I was quitting on my family back in the U.S, but most of all, I was ashamed because I felt I was quitting on my kids.

I almost made the biggest mistake anyone could have made, and many people counted on me to be there for them, especially my little ones. So I got into my car and started driving away. I started praying as I remembered all my loved ones and started begging God for His forgiveness while at the same time asking for His wisdom. I prayed the entire way back. I didn't even return to the office; I rushed home to see my kids.

When I got home, I immediately grabbed both of them in my arms and hugged them with all my strength and looked at both of them in their eyes, and I told them how much I loved them and how much they meant to me, in a way I was being thankful for what they had done for me at the cliff. As I hugged my kids and cried, I had a breakthrough moment when I came to realize that I desperately needed help, that I needed to get better for my kids and my family and so, I decided that I was going to seek assistance; I was not going to let whatever was happening to me to slowly ruin my life and the life of those people that were so important in my life.

It took me a couple of days to settle from what had happened at the cliff, but soon after, I started working and doing some research and finally found someone I could reach out to. The first person I talked to and visited was a family readiness counselor. On my first couple of visits, I would mostly just sit there in silence, but slowly, I started to trust her, and eventually, I opened up enough to have conversations about what was going on in my mind. After a few more visits, I finally told her about all these nightmares that kept coming back over and over, and she revealed to me that I could be suffering from Post-Traumatic Stress

Disorder (PTSD). This came to me as a complete shock as I never thought that I could be suffering from PTSD. The counselor then recommended that I make an appointment with a military psychiatrist to get suitable treatment for PTSD.

My visits with the psychiatrist were different but in a very positive way. On my first visit, I had to take a few tests that the doctor used to confirm that I was suffering from severe PTSD; I was immediately put in a treatment and recovery program. Every visit was excruciating as we discussed in great detail all the horrific things I had witnessed in Iraq. We discussed Jim and Todd a lot, the good and the bad, and how all this made me feel. The doctor helped me recognize certain trigger points and how to use breathing exercises to help me calm down every time I felt like I was having an anxiety attack. My psychiatrist put me on a path to help me regain my confidence, start trusting people again, and achieve my goals and chase my dreams.

Since that day at the cliff, my life has changed so much for the better. I retired from the military, and now I have a successful career working for one of the big federal agencies in the DC area. I also remarried the person I consider to be the love of my life, my wife; she has provided me with tremendous support to combat my PTSD. Thanks to her, I found a new hobby in bodybuilding, which helps me stay in shape both physically and mentally. We also form part of a combat veteran motorcycle riders association that works tirelessly to promote the well-being of all military service veterans who served our country by raising awareness on veteran's suicide and raising funds to help other veteran organizations achieve their mission of helping veterans. My kids are now almost all grown, and they continue to make me so proud of how smart and accomplished they are and the bright futures they have ahead. To them, I want to say "thank you" for being the guiding light and being the inspiration needed to get me to where I'm today.

As I sit here today, I feel like I have a new understanding of life. Life will continue, and it doesn't matter what is going on around you; life will continue to go on; you just have to give life a chance. Do not try to solve temporary problems with a "permanent and irreversible" solution. I learned that PTSD is a real disease that can happen to anyone, and if left untreated, it will consume you and kill you, just like a cancer. Seek help, talk to others, but also be on the lookout for others who may be suffering from this disease; it is ok to ask other people if they are fine. You never know, you could be saving a life. Finally, find that guiding light that will keep you focused on what really is important in life, and above all, pray and listen to God. I know healing from my invisible wound will take time, commitment, and continued effort, but I am determined to continue on my path to be a better son, brother, husband, and father.

About
Fabian Cardona

Fabian Cardona is an Air Force retired Master Sergeant who served 21.5 years. Currently, he is the Assistant Director of Mobile Assets for the Department of Homeland Security (DHS). Over his more than 25-year fleet management career, he has directed and supervised large and small federal fleets. Mr. Cardona successfully navigated the transition from vehicle technician to enterprise-wide fleet manager, and he possesses a combination of first-hand experience with a deep knowledge of vehicle and equipment technology and fleet management organization that is rare in the fleet management profession. Prior to joining DHS, he spent two years as a Senior Consultant for Mercury Associates, where he enabled Federal and local governments and corporate fleet managers to excel at their responsibilities. Prior to Mercury, he held positions as a service manager for Penske Truck Leasing and as program manager for a Department of Defense contracting agency, where he participated in the worldwide deployment of the Defense Property and Accountability System for the Air Force.

In his 21.5 years in the Air Force, he deployed twice to Iraq and twice to Afghanistan and served in multiple bases overseas. Fabian served as vehicle maintenance Superintendent and Installation Fleet Manager for various small and large fleets, where he led fleet maintenance programs with as many as 160 military and civilian maintenance technicians. He started his military career as a vehicle technician and ended it as a logistics and Fleet Management Advisor to general officers in CONUS and OCONUS (e.g., Afghanistan, Iraq) assignments.

Fabian is an avid volunteer in his community. He pairs his enthusiasm for riding motorcycles with his passion for helping others to raise awareness on Post Traumatic Stress Disorder, combat veteran homelessness, and war veteran suicide. He is a husband and a father of two kids, ages 17 and 19. He holds two Federal Fleet Manager Certifications, A Homeland Security Certificate, an associate degree in Applied Science in Vehicle Maintenance, a Bachelor of Arts in

Criminal Justice, and a Master of Arts in Management and Leadership.

Connect with Fabian Cardona

Email address: fcardona74@yahoo.com
Instagram: @mr._fabian

My Ring-Side Seat to Salvation
By William C. Scott

O h no, I'm home all by myself! Suddenly I had that sinking feeling in my stomach that you get when you come face to face with danger or trouble. I knew my wife and youngest son were gone to work, but I had just read my youngest daughter's text; this was her day off, and she was gone with friends for a girl's day out. That would not have been so bad, except I had just vomited four powerful blasts of what looked like coffee grounds, and I knew that was...not...good. Worst yet, immediately after I threw up, I felt dizzy, cold, hot, weak, and shaking, all simultaneously! I was also sweating and felt like I would pass out; it was as if my body were physically having a nervous breakdown or something. And while I was recovering, sitting on the bench holding on and hovering over the trash can, a weird thought crossed my mind; now I know how Macaulay Culkin from Home Alone felt - and I chuckled. This Wednesday morning was not starting out as a good day, and during my week off, no less! And this was just the beginning of a more turbulent journey that I would have preferred not to have taken on any day. But let me back up and tell you what led up to this moment.

The year 2016 was quite challenging for me. I had had enough, and this issue was beyond annoying and aggravating. Progressing from every now and then to basically every day was wearing on me, and I was over it. So, after conferring with my Primary Care Manager (PCM) at the Keesler Medical Center, he referred me to a gastroenterologist doctor. Doctor Gilkinson was very attentive to my situation, understanding of my frustrations, and wanted to help rid me of my swallowing complications. After an extensive discussion, Dr. G determined that the best plan of action was to perform an upper gastrointestinal (GI) procedure on me. She explained she would begin by exploring my esophagus, stomach, and small intestine to see if she could identify the problem. She also suggested that dilating my esophagus may be necessary as part of the solution. Of course, I'm nervous because this is uncharted waters for me. I have NEVER had anything snaked down my throat and into my belly – this is serious! However, because of Dr. G's calm demeanor and reassurance, she really put me at ease. So, she scheduled the procedure for two weeks later.

The big day arrived. After nurses had prepped and moved me to the operating room, the anesthesiologist announced the procedure, said my name, and I woke up in the recovery room. Dr. G stopped by and informed me that she could only go so far because there was still a small amount of food in my digestive tract that prevented her from going any further. I promised her I had fasted the required eight hours, and she assured me she did not doubt that I did. She explained to me that on occasion, this happens and could be part of the problem. And with that, she scheduled another procedure. Yay, more fasting, IV sticking, and throat gouging; I couldn't wait.

One week later, Dr. G. completed the second procedure successfully. She dilated my esophagus, took some biopsies, and then we waited for the lab results. A few days later, Dr. G. called and told me she needed blood drawn for more testing. When I inquired why she told me she saw an abnormal indication and needed further testing to verify the matter. She preferred to reserve judgment until she had more conclusive evidence. Now what I haven't told you up to this point is that the lab was becoming a familiar hangout for me. I had been dealing with high cholesterol for years with bi-annual checkups, and now pre-diabetes had crept in also. I was getting stuck all the time and just felt I could not get a break! My wife is cooking and eating everything she wants, and if I even peek at a fried pork chop, piece of chicken, or white rice, my readings are off the chart! Oh well, now I wait.

Hello. "Mr. Scott?"

"Yes."

"This is Dr. G calling from the GI clinic. I received your biopsies and lab results."

"Okay."

"Well, I'm afraid I have some unfortunate news."

"Really...okay."

"Yes. As I previously mentioned to you, I wanted to run more labs because of the abnormalities we saw; and the results show that you have...a carcinogenic tumor."

"Okay, so what does that mean in plain language?"

"Well, you have cancer...in your duodenum."

"In...my...what?"

"Your duodenum. It's the small area where the bottom of your stomach empties into your small intestine.

"Um-hmm...Sooo, where do we go from here?"

"Mr. Scott, I am so sorry that I had to share this diagnosis with you, but the good news is we've caught it early."

"Dr. G, you have no reason to apologize; it's not like you put it there. And you don't understand; this is a blessing in disguise; I didn't even come to you for this. If you had not found this now, there's no telling what the future outcome would be. So again, where do we go from here? "Well, first, we'll need to do some more tests to pinpoint a few things. Also, I'm assembling a team; this will include Oncology and surgery personnel. Because of the size of the tumor and where it's located, it's a good possibility it can be surgically removed. So, I will be scheduling appointments for you over the next few weeks. So, until you hear from me, take care of yourself, and I will talk with you soon. God bless"

Isn't it ironic how you can remember exactly where you were and what you were doing when a life-changing experience happened to you? I had stepped into the hallway from the classroom I was teaching in to take Dr. Gs' call. After saying our goodbyes, I ended the call and did what I knew best to do – pray. Right there in that hallway, I looked up toward heaven and said, "Lord, this is a situation that's totally out of my control. And you told me to cast my cares upon you because you care for me. So, Father, at this point, that's all I know to do. This is no longer my problem but yours, Lord. So, I'm just going to take me a ringside seat and watch you do what you do. And I'm thanking you in advance for healing me; however you decide to do it; in Jesus' name, Amen."

From there, I returned to my classroom and picked up where I left off.

When I got home, I told my wife Janice; we prayed and left it in the Lord's hands. We both had peace about it, and I can honestly say, neither fear, doubt, nor worry took residence among us. Looking back, I can also say I never asked God, why me? I saw this as a faith walk that God required me to walk out, trusting totally in him, each step of the way. Over the next two months, I endured numerous tests and injections leading up to the anticipated day of the surgery. I mentioned that I was going to take a ringside seat and watch God work; well, I did just that. The oncology team was great; Dr. Wright and his assistant immediately put me at ease, answering all my questions and reassuring me I was in the best of hands and would have the best care provided. Reflecting back, I WAS in the best hands – God embraced me and carried me totally through the process. And all along the way, He revealed everything to me that He was doing in my favor. When I first met my surgeon, Dr. Rojas, I had ten specific questions written down for him, which he answered to my satisfaction; but the last one was the most important one for me. I asked him directly if he believed in God.

He looked me right in the eye and in the most humble and sincere way said, "Mr. Scott, every time I walk into that operating room, I take God with me; I can't do it without him.' With a firm reassurance in my heart, I knew I had the right person on my team. While smiling, I extended my hand to him and joyfully welcomed him to the team.

After an MRI, two Octreoscans, and a CT scan, I was referred out to a hospital in Fairhope, Alabama, to have an upper Endoscopic Ultrasound (EUS) accomplished. This would determine if my surgery would be laparoscopic or if the surgeon would have to actually cut me open. Throughout this entire process, my family, friends, and church family were absolutely outstanding! There were so many words of encouragement, calls, and prayers on my behalf. The Sunday before my scheduled EUS, two brothers prayed for me when I went to the altar for prayer. At one point, Brother Terrence began pacing back and forth with tears streaming down his face, agonizing over whether he should tell me what God was showing him about my situation. Brother Stan finally interjected and said, "Just say it, brother!"

Terrence stepped to me, placed his hand on my abdomen, and said, "Scotty, God said that "No blade shall pierce your body."

My heart sank, and an overwhelming peace overshadowed me. I received that and left church thanking God for still showing himself faithful on my behalf while still in my ringside seat!

After the one hour and 20-minute drive to the referral hospital, the nurses were already waiting for me. During the prep, one particular nurse was raving about Dr. Eves. She proclaimed he was THE best GI doctor in the region, and after 12 years, they had finally got him in their hospital! On the drive over that morning, Janice mentioned that it would be a good day; as the nurse kept talking, I agreed with my wife and started smiling to myself – this was a setup by God, and my ringside seat was getting even more comfortable! When the doctor entered my room, it was easy to see the confidence he exhibited and the arrogancy he brandished. He briefed me on the procedure and then told me, "When I get in there, if I see it, I'm taking it out." This confused me a bit because, to my knowledge, he was only supposed to perform the EUS and send the results back to my team at Keesler so they could determine how to proceed next. I asked him if he could do that. He retorted, "When I get in there if I see it, I'm taking it out." He then departed the room, telling me he would see me in the OR.

When I woke up in the recovery room, Janice was at my side, and the nurse was removing my IV. Dr. E. came in and said, "Good news, you're now cancer-free." Janice and I looked at one another and then back at the doctor. "Did you say I'm cancer-free?" I asked. He replied, "I did. You are cancer-free. I told you, if I saw it, I was going to take it out. Now I need to see you back in two months for a follow-up to see how things are going." And with that, he was gone. During that surreal moment, it was nearly hard to believe, but Janice and I were elated and grateful. I dozed off during the ride home; after waking up and the words "cancer-free" resounding in my head, I thought maybe I had dreamed it all. I looked over to Janice and asked, "Did he say I'm now cancer-free?" Still driving and shaking her head in affirmation, she replied, "You are cancer-free." With that, I fell back asleep. On that Thursday, December 22nd, 2016, I had received an early Christmas gift – no more cancer. Merry Christmas to me, and no blade had pierced my body! God showed me what he was working with, while I enjoyed it all from my ringside seat!

That Friday morning, I woke up, and short of a sore throat, I felt fairly good. Earlier in the year, our daughters planned to come to the house and cook Christmas dinner (which is what I normally did). I agreed, told them to plan the menu, and I would buy the ingredients. With Christmas being just two days away, I didn't have any time to waste, and I still needed to finish my Christmas shopping. Although Janice protested, I was on a mission; I reassured her if I felt tired, I would cut it short and head home, and off I went. As grace would have it, the grocery and gift shopping went well. Although I wasn't done, I was getting a bit tired. So, I stopped for the day and headed home; besides, I still had tomorrow, Christmas Eve.

Saturday came and went; again, I got a bit tired, but mission accomplished – gift shopping finished! Janice fussed at me; she felt I was doing too much too soon. Sunday welcomed Christmas in, and after the previous two days of activities, I was feeling very thankful but a bit fatigued. After church, we exchanged gifts with the kids once they arrived, cooked (I eased in and helped a little before being chased out of the kitchen by Janice and the girls), ate, and relaxed for the rest of the evening. Besides feeling a bit fatigued, Monday went well, and since my youngest daughter was going to be off Tuesday & Wednesday, I suggested we go to the movies for family night.

Tuesday night at the movies started out fine, but mid-way through, I began feeling uncomfortable; I wasn't nauseated, but my core just didn't feel right. I spent the rest of the movie seeking a comfortable position, and I needed some relief by the end of the movie! After getting home, I discovered we had no Ginger Ale, but we had Mountain Dew. I reasoned that that would just have to do to settle my uneasiness; unfortunately, I realized that was not a smart move after only one mouthful. My daughter offered to go buy me some Ginger Ale, but I chose to go to bed instead to try sleeping it off. Then, from 3:30 to 4:30 AM., a storm erupted early morning mayhem by way of diarrhea with aggressively angry cramps. Finally, the privilege of peace and the reward of rest came my way, and I was able to sleep a few hours that morning.

Now, back to the future and on with Wednesday's turbulent journey. When we got home Tuesday night, there was a message on the answering machine (yes, we still had a landline phone) from Dr. R. He asked me to return his call to discuss our scheduled appointment for Thursday. After such a horrendous morning and finally getting back to sleep, I awakened at 8:00 AM; my priority was calling Dr. R. I grabbed my cell phone, headed into the kitchen, and replayed the message on the answering machine. Immediately after writing down the surgeon's phone number, I had a familiar feeling inside that warned me of trouble on the horizon. I had just enough time to grab the trashcan, and the fireworks began – those four powerful blasts of what looked like coffee grounds!

After finally gathering my faculties, I hoped the worst of the storm was over. Staring into the trashcan and trying to access what had just happened, again, I knew I was in trouble and needed help. At that very moment, the phone rang; the caller ID showed it was the doctor's office in Alabama. "Mr. Scott, this is Amy from Dr. Eve's office. How are you doing?" Funny you should ask, I replied. I just threw up four times in my trashcan, and it looks like coffee grounds. "Oh my. Hold on; I'm going to put you on hold," she said. About 30 seconds later, she returned to the phone and told me I was bleeding internally and needed to return immediately to the hospital in Alabama so they could find and fix the problem. I reminded her that I lived one and a half hours from the hospital, and with my wife at work, it would be a while before we got there. She told me she had to work on getting me a bed for admission, but I needed to get there as soon as possible. We then said our goodbyes.

I realized I was too weak to yell upstairs for my daughter, so I grabbed my cellphone to call her; that's when I saw her text; that's when I realized I was home alone and slowly fading– oh no! So, I attempted to call my wife at work – I got her voicemail; I called her cellphone - got her voicemail. I thought, "Okay, I need to call Dr. R to inform him we won't be meeting for my Thursday appointment since I was going to be admitted to the hospital in Alabama." When I called, I learned he was in surgery. I left a message and tried to contact Dr. G. to inform her; she was also in the Operating Room. "Great! Okay, what's going on? Where is everybody? Am I being punked?"

On another attempt, I finally reached my wife. After explaining the situation, she came home to get me. While she was en route, Dr. R. called. Once I explained everything, he instructed me not to go to Alabama but to come straight to the Keesler emergency room (a 20-minute drive). If necessary, they would transport me via ambulance to Alabama. When Janice arrived, I told her that after the morning I suffered I had to get a shower before leaving. She protested, but I did it anyway - boy was that a bad move! After nearly passing out and with no strength to call for help, I cried out to God for help; and he did. Upon arriving in the ER, it was the busiest I had ever seen; there was wall to wall people everywhere! Once I mentioned my internal bleeding, they rushed me back immediately. God was still working!

I endured a lot in the ER. I had to explain to four different doctors and two nurses my symptoms and my procedure in Alabama. They kept asking and trying to figure out what caused my bleeding while I repeatedly explained it. I persistently told them to call my GI doctor and surgeon, who was upstairs in the hospital and knew my history! After three hours, I finally persuaded them to call upstairs and talk to my GI doctor. All this was happening while my insides were still unsettled. I suffered through three IV sticks (one unsuccessful, and the nurse accused me of blowing my own vein out), and I was starving! Two technicians requested a stool sample in my room, and I told them that would be a very bad idea. I suggested they help me to a restroom and allow me to take care of that business in private; otherwise, with my unstable intestines. I would not be responsible for what would happen if they went back there.

After going to the restroom and providing them with the sample they needed, I returned to my room and finally saw a familiar face – Dr. Rojas. He explained everything to my wife, which put her more at ease; it wasn't his surgical skills I needed on the team, but his compassionate skills. Another dilemma was the fact that Dr. Eves' office had not sent my medical records to my Keesler team, so they had yet to see exactly what he did and what they needed to do. After eight hours in the ER and finally getting my records faxed from Alabama, my GI doctor determined I needed to spend the night in the ICU and have exploratory surgery the following day. And with that, I was moved into ICU and had a restful night's sleep. The next morning, even though the ICU staff was outstanding, I finally saw another familiar, smiling face – Dr. G., who took me in for exploratory surgery. When I awoke, she stopped by and gave me the great news - all bleeding stopped, and everything had ulcerated over, which was a good thing. She did not have to do anything and told me I should not have any more issues. After a three-day hospital stay, doctors released me on New Year's Eve. The next few weeks of recovery were challenging; I was weak and had no appetite, which I would later learn was due to me losing three liters of blood during that ordeal. And yet, God would not let Hell have me.

On January 1, 2017, I wrote this in my journal. "Father, you left me with a word leaving 2016 and then brought me into this new year with a confirmation of it." *For I know the plans I have for you, declares the Lord, plans to prosper you and not to harm you, plans to give you a hope and a future (an extended end). (Jeremiah 29:11).* "Thank you, Lord God, for reassuring me of your love for me, your care and provisions. You are great and greatly to be praised, and I give all that is within me to praise, honor, magnify and exalt you at all times!"

To this point, I'm not sure my story is indicative of a walk past hell. But this I do know; although my trauma may not appear traumatic to you, this is the hell I endured, and God granted me a ring-side seat to watch him deliver me through it. I am now five years cancer-free and thankful each day for my blessings. James 1:12 says, *"Blessed is the man who remains steadfast under trial, for when he has stood the test, he will receive the crown of life, which God has promised to those who love him."* While I still stand, God graciously continues to allow me a ring-side seat in His affairs in my life. What God brought me to, he brought me through; and I am forever grateful.

About
William C. Scott

Williams Scott is the co-founder and Vice President of Calling Men Back (CMB). Along with three other veterans, they established an organization designed to help men face challenges in their lives such as identity crisis, role responsibility and life purpose. The late Dr. Myles Munroe said, "Traditional roles once gave men stability and continuity from generation to generation. Today, the world is sending out conflicting signals about what it means to be a man." When Scotty (as he is affectionately called) read this, he reasoned within himself that some men need guidance as to how to

115

reclaim the roles and responsibilities for themselves, their families, and their communities. Scotty loves encouraging others, as noted by his fifth year of daily dissemination of Morning Motivational Messages, fondly referred to as M&Ms. Frustrated by all the newscasts and social media negativity, he determined within himself to promote positivity daily, beginning with his wife, children, friends and eventually many others.

This gospel preacher is a strong proponent of positive living. As both a cancer survivor and recent COVID survivor, he values life even more, seeking to learn something new each day. Scotty graduated Magna Cum Laude with a bachelor's degree in Multidisciplinary Studies from Grantham University. He was also an instructor for the Air Force teaching Radio Maintenance, Electronic Principles, Information Technology Fundamentals and Cyber Transport Systems for 16 years. This Civil Service employee currently serves as a Curriculum Development Manager for the Air Force continuing to develop training for future military students.

Scotty is a retired Air Force veteran who devoted 24 years of dedicated service to his country. He and his wife Janice have been married 40 years; they have 5 adult children and 3 grandchildren.

In his leisure time he enjoys fishing, watching mixed martial arts and playing racquetball.

William "Scotty" Scott. Veteran. Preacher. Encourager. Survivor.

Connect with William Scott
Email: scott284@bellsouth.net
Social Media: Facebook/William C Scott

God's Will For My Life
(Full Circle)
By Marcus Williams

I t was a typical Wednesday morning as I drove to my job. I worked at Ingalls Shipbuilders as a Senior Project Scheduler. I just had a new house built and purchased a new truck. I felt like things were going well in my life. Until one day, I was sitting at my desk when I received the phone call that would change the trajectory of my life. My sister says to me, "you need to come to the hospital to see Tony; he might not make it through the night."

Tony was one of my older brothers that I felt hated me. However, my older brothers were the only father figures in my life. They weren't perfect, but they showed me what a man should and shouldn't do. He was dying from cancer. My family was at his bedside.

I'm standing at the foot of the bed, and I say to him, "I love you, man." He can't talk, but he nods his head to let me know he loves me too. That's the last breath that he took. My mother screams, "my baby is gone," and falls into my arms. At that moment, I don't know how to feel. My mom is my world, and I don't know what to say to her to stop the pain. I can't understand her pain because, at this moment, I feel nothing. My world is crashing around me. Tony just died, and my oldest brother Tommy is walking up and down the hall to figure out how to function without

Tony. These two are best friends and brothers. My sister Vera is the backbone of the family, and she is losing it, and yet, I can't feel anything. I'm trying to be strong for my mom, but inside I'm devastated. This is one of the hardest times in my life, so I thought. It had been a very difficult week. We laid Tony to rest the following Saturday.

One week later, while still grieving over the death of my brother, I was at my desk working when I was called into my boss's office. He was there with his boss and two security guards! He then tells me, out of the blue, "This is your two weeks' notice. You do good work, but we're having a reduction in force, and we have to let you go."

He asked me did I have any questions or did I want to say anything. I guess I was in shock, but I told him no. He then asked me an odd question, "what are you going to do about your new truck now that you will be laid off?"

During this time, he and his boss were both standing there with the two-armed guards as if I was going to tear up the office or something. I didn't know what I was going to do. I'm thinking I have a wife and kids, a new house, a new truck, and NO job! So, I get back to the office and pack my belongings. I'm walking to my truck, trying to understand what just happened. I'm now in my truck driving home, and I'm asking myself, am I still the man of my house? Am I still a man at all? I had to then call and tell my wife everything that just happened. I'm feeling like a complete failure, but I didn't let on to her how I was feeling. She was already doing all she could to support me walking with me during this time. Inside I'm losing it. I don't know how I'm going to pay the bills, I'm grieving the loss of my brother, worried about my mom, but I still must put on a face as if everything was okay.

It was time for my Tuesday night small group meeting, Band of Brothers, with other men from my church. The Bible says, "Iron sharpens Iron, so one person sharpens another." (Proverbs 27:17). During this time, I felt like I couldn't sharpen anything or anyone. I believed I didn't deserve to try to help anybody when I couldn't even take care of my own family. I felt I couldn't protect or take care of my wife. What could I offer to the brothers? I wasn't sleeping at all; bills were piling up, I was hiding my truck in the garage so that it wouldn't get repossessed. So, I'm feeling like a hypocrite coming to these meetings, not understanding who I am at this point. I felt like my family would be better off without me.

After the meeting, I received a call from my brothers of CMB (Calling Men Back), William Scott and Eric Ward, who noticed I was not my usual jolly self. They asked me was I okay, and all I could tell them was if I had one bullet, everything would be fine. They told me not to allow myself to think like that. I couldn't understand how my life shifted so far after one phone call. I also mentioned in the small group that I thought about driving my truck off the bridge. At the time, I thought that would fix everything, not thinking at all about what that would do to my family.

A short time after that meeting, one of the brothers in the group approached and asked me what it would take to turn things around. My mind was so cloudy with failure and doubt by now; I could hardly see straight. I told him that I needed $1500 to take a class for certification in New Orleans. With this certification, I could get a better job and try to make things better for my family. This brother told me he believed in me and gave me the money! He then says to me, "Go and do what you need to for your family."

I didn't understand why anyone would take a chance like that on me. He really didn't know me, and I didn't want to seem like I was begging are anything. I did not yet recognize God's hand all in the mix! He was lining it all up! *And we know that all things work together for the good to them that love God, to them that are called according to his purpose.* (Romans 8:28)

I took the class, and I got the certification, but still, nobody would hire me! I was feeling less than a man but trying to keep up a front so people would think I have it all together. Because this is what I thought a man was supposed to do. I had just seen God's hand move, but the rejection I felt was trying to cloud my vision. After a few weeks of faking and acting like all was well in our lives so people could talk about how well we were doing, I finally received a phone call. It was a job offer, but it was 17 hours away in Pittsburgh, PA! I'm thinking this could be a setback because there was no way my wife was going to agree to me leaving or moving that far away. So, I told the people I needed to talk to my wife, and I would call them back.

When I hung up the phone, I told God, "If this is YOUR WILL for my life and my family, my wife would be okay with it, and I will take this job."

So, I told my wife, she said, "let's pray about it." We prayed. We asked God for His will to be done in this situation and to please lead and guide us. We also asked for a miracle because I needed money for me to get to Pittsburg. I would also need money for a hotel and money for gas to get there. Through the years, I had applied for my military service connection. I had been rejected by them so many times. It actually wasn't at the forefront of my mind. But things were about to change. With everything that had been going on, it seemed that finally, we got a breakthrough! My phone rang one day, and my wife was on the other end screaming, praising God. She told me that ten thousand dollars was just put into our account! I had finally received money from the military service connection due to my PTSD. This was exactly what we needed! I knew without a doubt that this was the absolute hand of God! My wife was in agreement, and things were starting to turn around. My vision was starting to become clear because I could see that our answer came after we prayed. I saw the scripture come to fruition, *But seek ye first the Kingdom of God and his righteousness and all these things will be added unto you* (Matthew 6:33).

So, we were preparing for me to leave, and I went to church that last Sunday with my wife. All was well until a visitor asked me if she could pray for me. She had heard that I was about to take a job out of state that would separate me from my wife. After telling her she could pray for me, she said to me, "a house divided won't stand."

I stopped her and said, "My house isn't divided because my wife and I both agreed with God's will for our family." I didn't want to be rude, but I stopped her from praying for me because I didn't agree with her.

At that moment, God asked me a question, "Whose voice will you listen to?" I had to take a stand and not allow someone to try to kill or destroy God's plan for my life. I realize she meant well, but I decided to follow God. I was starting to see that this was indeed God's will for us. The enemy was trying to hinder God's plan for my life. The scripture says t*he thief comes only to kill, steal and destroy. I have come that they may have life and have it to the full* (John 10:10).

With everything that had taken place in my life, when I got to Pittsburg alone, I realized that God had to get me away from everybody so he could show me some things. Most of my life, I would ask why didn't my father want me? What did I do to make him not want me? What could I do to get him to say, I'm proud of you, and I love you? God answered those questions, and He showed me how He saw me. He had to get me in a place where I couldn't hide behind my wife, spiritual brothers, or anyone else. God had to show me that He had ordered my steps. He opened my eyes so I could see what he wanted me to see and understand what he needed me to do. I realized that there was truly a Calling on my life, but I needed to get to a place where I could hear him better. Psalm 46:10 says, *be still and know that I am God.*

I was away from home for a year and a half. During that time, there were many conversations with God. He showed me so many things about myself. A short time later, my oldest brother became extremely sick and unexpectedly died in his home. Once again, I'm having to lean hard into God and ask for his guidance. My already grieving mother had to bury another son. However, this time I felt that God had somehow prepared me for this. I understood better who I was and how to maneuver in times like this for my family.

At the same time, my job in Pittsburgh was ending due to contractual issues. Since it was seventeen hours away, my wife and I had already prayed that I would get a job closer to home. I had been searching for other jobs, then miraculously, a job closer to home was offered to me, and it was in St. Louis where my mother resided! This was ten hours away, instead of seventeen! The call that I received was from the Army Corp of Engineers asking to interview over the phone. I was told during that call that I would get an answer in a week or two. Instead, they called me back in two days, asking me to come to St. Louis for an in-person interview. I'm thinking, well, at least I would get a free trip to St. Louis and see my mom and family. After the interview, I talked to my wife, and she told me if I had a chance to be close to my mom, I should take the job if offered. She told me that even though she wanted me at home, she knew my mom was now grieving two sons and needed me more. I was offered the job, and I took it.

My wife and I felt that this was definitely the hand of God because my mother needed to heal, and she wanted her last living son to be with her. I ended up staying a year and a half in St. Louis with my mom and sister. During that time, I had some of the most incredible opportunities. My sister is very active in her community and is always attending important meetings. She introduced me to some very great men that ended up mentoring me and encouraging me to pursue the things that God had placed in my heart. I became a part of the St. Louis Mayoral Candidate team. The things I learned, the networking, and the connections I made there were all a part of God's plan.

One Friday, I came home from work; momma told me it's time for you to go home now and be the husband, father, friend, and leader that God has called you to be. My mother had no idea that I was one of the founders of Calling Men Back. She knew what God had put in me, and she believed that if I continued to stay in the will of God, I could do anything. After living in St. Louis for a year and a half, it was time for me to get back home to my wife. Now that I've been blessed to come out on the other side of this very long and hard journey, I realized that God had to move me out of my own way, so I could see my life the way he saw it. Now I have come full circle, from wanting to drive my truck off the bridge, asking for one bullet, to talking to young men and helping them understand who they are —

teaching them that God created them with a purpose in mind and they should ask Him for guidance. I now have the opportunity to join in with other men as we show the younger men that they too can be effective, successful, and influential in their families, neighborhoods, and their communities. This is what I know that God has called me to do. *Commit yours works to the Lord, and your plans will be established* (Proverbs 16:3).

About
Marcus Williams

M arcus Williams is originally from Chicago, IL and later moved to the Mississippi Gulf Coast in the 1980's. He graduated from Pascagoula High School in 1988. He enlisted and went into the Army straight out of high school. He honorably served six years in the U.S. military. Marcus is a member of Temple Lodge #98 and Tennessee Valley Consistory Lodge #160 in Huntsville, AL. He is also a member of Knights Templar in Birmingham, AL.

Marcus has worked for companies such as Huntington Ingalls Shipyard as Production Planner/Scheduler, Westinghouse Nuclear Power Plant as Project Controls Lead Scheduler/Planner, and MK Industries as CPM Scheduler. He is currently employed by the US Army Corp of Engineers, St. Louis District as Project Scheduler.

Not only is he a man of God but is also the co-founder and President of Calling Men Back (CMB), an organization designed to help men face challenges in their lives such as identity crisis, role responsibility and life purpose.

When Marcus is not working and mentoring men, he is spending time with his family. He is a loving husband, father, and friend.

Connect with Marcus Williams
Website: www.callingmenbackllc.com
E-mail: cmb.wawg@yahoo.com

Made in the USA
Middletown, DE
24 May 2022

66163605R00076